Discovering Fossils

How to Find and Identify Remains of the Prehistoric Past

FRANK A. GARCIA & DONALD S. MILLER

with illustrations by Jasper Burns

STACKPOLE BOOKS

0 11557 02800 3

Published by
STACKPOLE BOOKS
5067 Ritter Road
Mechanicsburg, PA 17055

Printed in the United States of America
10 9 8 7 6 5 4 3 2 1
First edition

Cover design by Wendy A. Reynolds
Composition by Doric Lay Publishers

The following illustrations were reprinted with the permission of the Virginia Museum of Natural History: p. 98, *Myliobatis* sp.; p. 103, *Striatolamia macrota, Notorhynchus primigenius*; p. 105, *Galocerdo contortus*; p. 108, *Thecachampsa* sp.; p. 170, *Neuropteris scheuchzeri*; p. 174, *Cyrtospirifer disjunctus*; p. 176, *Spinocyrtia granulosa*; p. 177, *Cucullea gigantea*; p. 178, *Placopecten clintonius, Turritella mortoni*; p. 179, *Cadulus* sp.; p. 181, *Hercoglossa twomeyi*; p. 185, *Pentremites* sp.; p. 188, *Phacops rana*.

Library of Congress Cataloging-in-Publication Data

Garcia, Frank A.
    Discovering fossils : how to find and identify remains of the
  prehistoric past / Frank A. Garcia & Donald S. Miller : with
  illustrations by Jasper Burns. — 1st ed.
          p.   cm.
    Includes bibliographical references and index.
    ISBN 0-8117-2800-5 (alk. paper)
    1. Fossils—Collection and preservation. I. Miller, Donald S.
  (Donald Stuart), 1953– . II. Title.
  QE718.G37   1998
  560' .75—dc21   97–32171
                                                      CIP

To those with the spirit and love for discovering our past, being the first to bring to light, at any cost, the miracle of fossils.

Contents

PART TWO   FOSSIL IDENTIFICATION

APPENDICES

Acknowledgments

I wish to acknowledge the following people, who have deeply affected my life and my love of fossils:

My grandfather, Duncan Padgett, who lit the fire of fossiling for me on the banks of Lake Okeechobee in 1954.

Dr. S. David Webb, of the University of Florida, one of the world's most revered paleontologists, who was my mentor.

Dr. Russ McCarty, of the University of Florida, whose expertise in fossil preparation is exceeded only by his kindness.

Dr. Clayton Ray, who believed in me enough to ask me to work as a collaborator with the Smithsonian Institution, and who once told me that he was "not interested in degrees, but results."

Dr. Daryl P. Domning, of Howard University and research associate at the Smithsonian Institution, who was the prime individual I worked for as he undertook one of the most important studies of the history of fossil sirenians and who, along the way, became a very dear friend.

Mr. Robert Purdy, of the Department of Paleobiology at the Smithsonian Institution.

Howard H. Converse, Jr., whose expertise helped me in learning about fossil preparation and in the pursuit to be the best at anything.

Bud Leisey, Jane Leisey Hunter, and Eric Hunter for their unselfish acts and support of one of the greatest paleontological projects in the world, the Leisey Shell Pit fossils, and the Caloosa Shell Company, managed by William "Bill" Casey, his lovely wife, LeAnn, and their super son, Craig.

Don Wilson, of Wilson Excavations in Sarasota, Florida, who gives unselfishly of his time and effort. Both Bill Casey and Don Wilson are top supporters of The Paleontological Education Preserve.

Special thanks to Jack and Debbie Weldon and Ernie Kendler, who are the fire and drive behind The Paleontological Education Preserve.

Larry Isaacs, Larry Peace, Janet Roth, Sam Marshall, Joe Shaw, Diane Yomans, Ginny Germond, and Diane Stephanie of IMC Fertilizer, Inc., who made it possible for me to frequent their company's properties to more fully uncover and understand the paleontological story of Florida's phosphate region.

Austin Cargill, Gray Gordon, Joyce Bodie, Jack Schmedeman, Ron Brownlow, Carol Moye, Christine Smith, and Brenda Menendez of Cargill Fertilizer, Inc. for allowing me access to their properties in my quest to further advance the story of prehistoric sirenians.

I wish to thank my lovely wife, Dixie Miller Garcia, Kyle and Monica Gannarelli, my three "old" best friends, Don Ward, John Clark, and Ron Shrader, Junior Fowler, Steve Beck, Mickey Fowler, Ben Waller, Sue and Jim Pendergraft, Charlie and Sue Bodishbaugh, Rudi Johnson, Red Tincher, Bob Baine, Tony Estevez, D. J. Bethea, Margaret Stallard, Henry Bonar, Bob Hite, Bill Campbell, John Eastman, Bob Fellows, Joe Guidry, Kurt Loft, Bernard Shaw, John Zarella, and Bryant Gumble for their tireless efforts and support of the Leisey Shell Pit project. Also Milton and Wilma Arner, Steve and Diane Arner and their children Chadd and Nikki, Merlin and Roberta Kesselring, Marle and Laurine Smith, Wes and Gerri Pettipiece, Grace and Alan Wiland, Larry Rotolo, and Lester Huckaby. Also, a special thanks to Congressman Sam Gibbons and Senator Bob Graham for their support of my work with the children.

A very warm thank-you goes to my coauthor, Don Miller, without whom this book would not have been written. He has found his niche in life as a wonderful writer and literary researcher.

I want to thank Jasper Burns, our illustrator. Though we've not met in person, I feel I know him from his wonderful artwork and perhaps because he is related to my hero, Thomas Jefferson.

I wish to thank my mothers, Hilda and Joy, my dads, Charlie and Albert, and finally, my beautifully talented and wonderful daughter, my little girl, Amy Garcia Little.

—*Frank Garcia*

To begin with, I wish to thank a woman I will never get to meet, Katheryne Whittemore. She taught a physiography course that my mother took at Buffalo State Teachers College in the early 1930s. As a result, my mother developed an appreciation for fossils, although it was not acted upon until many years later.

I want to thank my mother and father, Bess and Milton Miller, not only for being my parents, but also for planning a family outing to Maryland's Calvert Cliffs to collect fossil shark teeth on a cold and blustery March day in 1963. I became hooked on fossils that day and have been ever since.

Thanks go to Ed Lauginiger for reviewing the first draft of this book, to Cynthia Miller for reviewing the first draft and generously lending fossil specimens for the identification section, and to Gene Hartstein for his review and input.

I also wish to thank Daryl P. Domning, Professor of Anatomy at Howard University, and David C. Parris, Curator at the New Jersey State Museum, for their review and helpful comments. Any remaining factual or conceptual errors are, of course, my responsibility.

Jasper Burns, whose magnificent artwork graces this book, unknowingly generated the impetus that resulted in this book. He was "the friend I hadn't met" until we began this adventure.

I also wish to thank my coauthor, Frank Garcia, for his unparalleled contributions to the science of paleontology. Just as important, his excitement and enthusiasm about fossils are more infectious than the Ebola virus.

My appreciation also goes to Sally Atwater, formerly of Stackpole Books, Jane Devlin, and all of the people at Stackpole who worked with us to produce the best book possible. I also wish to thank my literary agents, Mike Larsen and Elizabeth Pomada.

Finally, I thank Deva Scheel, who tolerated my fossil exploits in the early years and later came to understand and appreciate them, and my wonderful daughter, Julia Miller, who is my biggest booster and is responsible for my returning to fossil collecting as an adult.

—*Don Miller*

About the Authors

Frank A. Garcia is responsible for more than 30 previously undiscovered species of prehistoric animals and is widely acknowledged as one of the greatest fossil hunters of all time. His most important contribution to paleontology is his discovery and subsequent excavation of the Leisey Shell Pit site in Ruskin, Florida—one of the richest and most important early Ice Age fossil sites in the world. Since 1985, he has introduced more than 40,000 schoolchildren to the thrill of discovering fossils. He lives in Ruskin, Florida.

Donald S. Miller is a fossil collector, writer, and proprietor of Miller's Fossils, Inc., a supplier of fossils and natural history items to institutions, museums, and individuals throughout the United States and Canada. He lives in Wilmington, Delaware.

Jasper Burns is an artist, writer, and fossil collector. He is the author and illustrator of *Fossil Collecting in the Mid-Atlantic States* (Johns Hopkins University Press, 1991). He lives in Charlottesville, Virginia.

Preface

Fossils and the study of prehistoric life have been sources of wonder and amazement for thousands of years, from Stone Age people whose remains are found with fossil teeth, bones, and shells, to the ancient Greeks, to Thomas Jefferson, the first fossil collector in the White House, to an eight-year-old who can debate theories of dinosaur extinction with the best of the professionals. Yet paleontology, the branch of science that seeks to describe and understand prehistoric life, is only about two hundred years old. As a result, there is still much more to learn.

Paleontology brings together people with interests in various fields such as geology, zoology, botany, climatology, anatomy, physiology, chemistry, genetics, and animal behavior. Understanding the story of life on earth requires a great deal of knowledge about many things.

But if you ask any Ph.D., serious amateur, or casual collector how they got interested in fossils, their response invariably starts with "Well, when I was a kid . . ." In fact, if you scratch beneath the surface of any adult with even a passing interest in fossils, you'll still find that kid. And that is the true secret of what attracts millions of people around the world to fossils: Discovering and learning about *really* old things keeps you young.

Each of us may be drawn to a different time period or a different kind of plant or animal. We may wax enthusiastic about Cambrian trilobites, Devonian corals, dinosaurs, sharks, or saber-toothed cats, but all fossil enthusiasts hear something that other people don't: We hear the voices of past times and past lives in these ancient rocks.

Our responses may be different. Some of us respond to the beauty, the mystery, the search for understanding, or the thrill of the hunt and the excitement of discovery. But in the end, we all go about it the same way: We go out into nature, pick up some rocks, and bring them home.

This book is written to help you find, identify, and understand those rocks with voices so that you too may someday have the kind of take-your-breath-away adventures that we've experienced.

PART ONE

What You Should Know before You Go

Geologic Time

The story of life on earth is one that stretches across a span of time so long as to be virtually unimaginable, even to the professional paleontologist. It is generally believed that the earth was formed about 4.5 billion years ago. Since then, countless changes in the earth's geography, climate, atmospheric composition, and biodiversity have occurred. This time, from 4.5 billion years ago to the present, is called geologic time.

In an effort to bring some order and understanding to these changes, scientists have developed a time scale that divides geologic time into meaningful periods of time based on climatic and geologic changes, periods of new life forms, and mass extinctions. Keep in mind, however, that although scientists have written that an era, period, or epoch lasted for a specific number of years, the truth is that these delineations are not really that clear. Nature takes its time about things, and transitions from one time period to another may have taken hundreds of thousands of years.

In a kind of geologic shorthand, the time from the formation of the earth to about 570 million years ago is referred to as Precambrian time. It encompasses approximately 87 percent of the history of the earth, from the formation of the planet to the time when marine organisms with hard parts such as shells and exoskeletons appeared in great numbers. The geologic time scale from 570 million years ago up to the present includes three *eras*, each of which is broken down into *periods*. The two most recent periods are further subdivided into *epochs*. We can all imagine what the world must have been like back then, but for the purposes of this book,

GEOLOGIC TIME

	Millions of Years	
	Begin–End	Elapsed Time
Cenozoic era	**65–present**	
Quaternary period	1.7–present	
Holocene epoch	0.01–present	
Pleistocene epoch	1.7–0.01	1.69
Tertiary period	65–1.7	63.3
Pliocene epoch	5–1.7	3.3
Miocene epoch	24–5	19
Oligocene epoch	37–24	13
Eocene epoch	58–37	21
Paleocene epoch	65–58	7
Mesozoic era	**245–65**	**180**
Cretaceous period	144–65	79
Jurassic period	208–144	64
Triassic period	245–208	37
Paleozoic era	**570–245**	**325**
Permian period	286–245	41
Pennsylvanian period	320–286	34
Mississippian period	360–320	40
Devonian period	408–360	48
Silurian period	438–408	30
Ordovician period	505–438	67
Cambrian period	570–505	70
Precambrian era	**4,500–570**	**3,930**

we let it go at that—imagination. However, sometime, somewhere, life began. Elements, molecules, and compounds combined in many ways until one combination produced that fateful spark of life that eventually led to you reading this book.

PRECAMBRIAN ERA

The oldest direct evidence of life comes from microscopic fossils collected from Australia of both bacterial and algaelike forms. These fossils are about 3.5 billion years old, and therefore, life must have begun sometime before then.

The oldest fossils in North America come from the shores of Lake Superior in western Ontario. These are microfossils similar to blue-green algae that date to nearly 2 billion years ago. Chemical analysis indicates that photosynthesis may have been taking place by this time.

In 1-billion-year-old rocks from the Northern Territory of Australia, a number of species of organisms have been described similar to blue-green algae, colonial bacteria, fungi, and green algae. By this time, it appears that the nucleus of the cell had developed.

Fossils from South Australia indicate that by 700 million years ago, soft-bodied organisms such as worms and jellyfish had evolved with tissue structures. Sometime between 700 million and 570 million years ago, hard parts such as shells and outer skeletons developed. At this point, the fossil record begins to show the remains of distinct body parts.

PALEOZOIC ERA

Cambrian Period

The Cambrian period is the oldest of the seven geologic periods of the Paleozoic era. Cambria was the Roman name for Wales, where rocks from this period were first described. The Cambrian period lasted 65 million years, from 570 million to 505 million years ago. Its most distinctive features were a near explosion in the number of fossils with hard parts and the progressive change in the atmosphere from what we consider toxic gas to an oxygen-rich atmosphere.

Most of the land surface was joined together in a large continent called Gondwana. A much smaller continent, called Laurentia, also existed, encompassing most of present-day North America. Northwestern Africa, as part of Gondwana, was centered over the south magnetic pole, leaving the Northern Hemisphere virtually covered by ocean.

Among the most plentiful fossils from the Cambrian period are trilobites, three-lobed marine invertebrates with an exoskeleton. Although many other forms have been described, they are not as well understood.

In the United States, outcrops of Cambrian age can be found in a narrow band from New England to Mississippi, throughout northern Wisconsin, in isolated points from New Mexico north to the Canadian border, and in the Black Hills of South Dakota.

Ordovician Period

The Ordovician period lasted 67 million years, from 505 million to 438 million years ago. Its name comes from a Celtic tribe, the Ordovices, who lived in the area of Wales where rocks of this period were first studied in detail.

The climate warmed early in the period but cooled toward the end. North America was covered by shallow seas for most of this period. The diversity of organisms rose quickly and dramatically at the beginning of the period but fell toward the end, probably due to global cooling. This was the first of the five major mass extinctions in earth's history.

Trilobites were abundant, but shelled fauna such as brachiopods (shellfish usually attached to the seafloor), gastropods (snails), and pelecypods (bivalves) became numerous. Nautiloids (imagine an octopus in a straight or coiled shell), corals, and crinoids (sea lilies) became established. Jawless fish, the first vertebrates, appeared during this period.

Ordovician outcrops in the United States follow the Cambrian pattern but can also be found more plentifully in New York State and parts of the Midwest.

Silurian Period

The Silurian period lasted for 30 million years, from 438 million to 408 million years ago. The name comes from another Celtic tribe, the Silures, who once lived in the region of Wales where these rocks were first described.

No new invertebrate groups appeared, but both vertebrates and plants showed major developments. Jawless fish became more abundant, and true fish first appeared. The earliest authenticated land plants also made their first appearance. Eurypterids (sea scorpions) and crinoids flourished. As in the Ordovician period, North America was generally covered by a warm and shallow sea.

Silurian outcrops occur along the Mississippi River and points east, primarily in the Great Lakes region, New York, and the mid-Atlantic Appalachian region.

Devonian Period

The Devonian period, or the Age of Fish, lasted for 48 million years, from 408 million to 360 million years ago. The name was derived from the county of Devonshire in southwestern England, where these rocks were first studied.

A number of major changes occurred in plant, invertebrate, and vertebrate forms. Land plants began to show great diversification, and the first forests appeared. The major marine invertebrate development was the appearance of the goniatites, which were the precursors of the ammonites, similar to coiled nautiloids but with more intricate shell structures. The first spiders and insects evolved. Jawless fish all but disappeared by the end of the period, leaving only lampreys and hagfish as their descendants. The sheer number of cartilaginous fish, such as sharks and rays, and bony fish grew dramatically. Toward the end of the period, amphibians, having evolved from fish, began to walk on land. The Devonian ended with the second of the major mass extinctions. The eastern United States was generally covered by water, but most of the West was dry.

Devonian outcrops occur in the mid-Atlantic Appalachians, New York, parts of the Great Lakes region, the Rocky Mountain states, and parts of Texas and New Mexico.

Carboniferous Period

The Carboniferous period, or the Age of Amphibians, lasted for 74 million years, from 360 million to 286 million years ago. It was during this period that most of the world's coal deposits were laid down. In North America, the Carboniferous is divided into two periods. The *Mississippian Period,* named for the marine limestones laid down at this time in the Mississippi Valley, lasted 40 million years, from 360 million to 320 million years ago. The *Pennsylvanian Period,* named for the coal deposits formed in that state, lasted 34 million years, from 320 million to 286 million years ago.

Early in the Carboniferous, much of North America was inundated by a warm and shallow sea which supported abundant plant life, invertebrates, and fish. Insects flourished in this hot and humid environment. Marine invertebrates, such as crinoids, brachiopods, and corals, were abundant. Fish thrived, as did the early amphibians. The seas became quite shallow, forming coastal lakes and lagoons, which supported huge, forested swamps. The resultant vegetation collected, rotted, turned into peat, and eventually became coal. Toward the end of the Carboniferous, the first true land animals, the reptiles, evolved from the amphibians.

Outcrops of both Mississippian and Pennsylvanian deposits occur widely throughout the middle and upper Midwest and in the Appalachians. Pennsylvanian outcrops occur in the Rocky Mountain states as well.

Permian Period

The Permian period was the last period of the Paleozoic era and lasted 41 million years, from 286 million to 245 million years ago. It was named after the province of Perm in Russia. In contrast to the Carboniferous, the Permian was characterized by a more arid climate. In marine environments, brachiopods and bivalves were common, the ammonites evolved rapidly, and the belemnites (squidlike animals with bullet-shaped internal guards) first appeared.

The real story in the Permian, however, occurred on land. Amphibians became less abundant because of drier conditions, but the reptiles developed dramatically, leading to two important lines. The mammal-like reptiles, exemplified by the sail-backed *Dimetrodon,* ruled the land while a second group of reptiles, the archosaurs, lurked in their shadow.

The third, and most devastating, incidence of mass extinction in earth's history marked the end of the Permian. Nearly 90 percent of all species became extinct. This included all trilobites and many bony fish, sharks, and land plants. The mammal-like reptiles virtually disappeared, but their small, hairy descendants survived the next 160 million years under the footsteps of the descendants of the archosaurs, the dinosaurs. By the end of the Permian, almost all land masses had drifted together into one supercontinent called Pangea.

In the United States, Permian outcrops occur almost exclusively west of the Mississippi.

MESOZOIC ERA

Triassic Period

The Mesozoic era is generally referred to as the Age of Reptiles. The Triassic period was the oldest of the three geologic periods of the Mesozoic era and lasted for 37 million years, from 245 million to 208 million years ago. The Triassic was so named for the three-part sequence in which rocks of this age occurred in southern Germany. During the Triassic, the climate was generally warm and dry. Triassic deposits usually consist of reddish sandstone and mudstone, testifying to the more arid climate.

The seas were warm, and coral, echinoderms, belemnites, and ammonites were the major members of the invertebrate fauna. Bony fish were plentiful, but sharks were not. On land, ferns, cycads, and conifers grew on the northern part of the North American continent, whereas seed ferns predominated on the southern part. Although the first true mammals appeared during the Triassic, the period belonged to the reptiles. The first dinosaurs walked the land, the first pterosaurs sailed the skies, and the first ichthyosaurs, plesiosaurs, and turtles swam the oceans. The Triassic ended with the fourth major mass extinction.

In the eastern United States, Triassic outcrops occur in a narrow band from the Connecticut Valley (famous for numerous dinosaur track sites), through New Jersey and Pennsylvania, and down to North Carolina. Triassic outcrops are scattered throughout the West. Perhaps the most famous Triassic site in the world is the Petrified Forest in Arizona.

Jurassic Period

The Jurassic period, named for the Jura Mountains on the border of France and Switzerland, lasted for 64 million years, from 208 million to 144 million years ago. The seas were warm and supported numerous ichthyosaurs, plesiosaurs, ammonites, belemnites, and shellfish. The first modern sharks appeared during this period.

The Jurassic climate was predominantly mild and subtropical. There was sufficient rainfall to support lush vegetation and heavy forests, which were widespread across most land areas. Some dinosaurs grew to tremendous size, as evidenced by huge sauropod herbivores, such as the 87-foot-long *Diplodocus,* and carnivores, such as the 35-foot-long *Allosaurus.* The lush vegetation supported more than one thousand species of insects. The first birds appeared, as represented by *Archaeopteryx.* The mammal-like reptiles were now extinct, as were most amphibians.

In the United States, Jurassic outcrops occur primarily west of the Mississippi, although some are found in New Jersey and Pennsylvania.

Cretaceous Period

The Cretaceous period, named for the chalk (Latin, *creta*) that was laid down in parts of what are now Europe and North America during this time, was the last of the Mesozoic periods. It spanned 79 million years, from 144 million to 65 million years ago, and probably ended with a bang—perhaps a very big bang. Current thinking holds that a large asteroid crashed near the Yucatan Peninsula of Mexico, initiating the process that began or ended the last of the five major mass extinctions. Approximately 65 percent of all species became extinct, including all dinosaurs, all flying reptiles, many marine reptiles, and small marine organisms, as well as the ammonites.

In the initial part of the Cretaceous, the warm, semitropical climate continued; however, both the geography and the climate changed during the last 30 million years, as extensive submersion of land areas occurred and the chalk deposits were laid down. North America was divided by a vast, warm sea stretching from the Gulf of Mexico to the Canadian Northwest Territories.

In the seas, the ammonites and other invertebrates declined and then became extinct. Large marine reptiles such as the ichthyosaurs, plesiosaurs, and mosasaurs (huge sea lizards that first appeared in the Cretaceous) all became extinct. Conversely, many modern bony fish, sharks, crocodiles, turtles, and some amphibians first appeared during this period and survived.

On land, flowering plants began to take hold. The duck-billed dinosaurs replaced the sauropods as the primary herbivores. The armored dinosaurs replaced plated dinosaurs. The horned dinosaurs first appeared and became numerous. The carnosaurs (carnivorous dinasaurs) reached their zenith in North America with *Tyrannosaurus rex*. All dinosaurs became extinct at the end of the Cretaceous. The flying reptiles also became extinct, although the birds survived and went on to flourish. Most important, the furry little mammals that lived under the dinosaurs' feet for 160 million years made it through the mass extinction. (And thank goodness; otherwise, there would be no one to read this book.)

Cretaceous outcrops appear in a small area of the mid-Atlantic states, a band through the Southeast, and extensively in the plains and Rocky Mountain states.

CENOZOIC ERA

The Cenozoic era, or the Age of Mammals, spans the time from the end of the Cretaceous period up to modern times. The Cenozoic is divided into two periods, and because the fossil record is more abundant and better understood, these periods are further subdivided into epochs. Earlier periods are also subdivided, but in different ways.

Tertiary Period

The Tertiary period was the first period of the Cenozoic era and lasted approximately 63 million years, from 65 million until 1.7 million years ago. The Tertiary is subdivided into five epochs, whose names are derived from Greek root words.

The *Paleocene epoch* (meaning "old recent life") lasted only 7 million years, from 65 million to 58 million years ago, but witnessed a major change on land and in the sea. The Paleocene is best noted for the explosion of flowering plants and mammals, which filled the void left by the extinction of the dinosaurs. Sea levels dropped, thereby changing worldwide geography and climate.

In the oceans, new forms of gastropods and bivalves replaced the ammonites as the primary marine invertebrates. Sharks became prolific, and bony fish also thrived. Mammals—both herbivores and carnivores—evolved quickly, with a wide range in size. Lemurlike primates first appeared. Birds diversified quickly, with some flightless, carnivorous species reaching over 6 feet in height.

The *Eocene epoch* ("dawn of recent life") lasted 21 million years, from 58 million to 37 million years ago. It was a time of continental plate activity and rising sea levels. North America was finally separated from Europe by the Atlantic Ocean, and the climate was either tropical or temperate in most land areas.

In the oceans, nautiloids thrived, and cuttlefish and crabs began to show a modern appearance. Some mammals returned to the sea and evolved into the first whales and sea cows. The whales thrived and evolved quickly, with some reaching lengths of 50 feet. Modern-appearing freshwater fish became abundant. The fish fossils of the Green River formation in Wyoming demonstrate the diversity and sheer numbers of fish in this prehistoric lake environment.

Many modern birds first appeared during this epoch, including ducks, geese, herons, owls, and hawks. Insects flourished, which benefited flowering plants, as insects became the major vehicle for pollination.

Mammals diversified dramatically, as some early "experimental" types became extinct and were replaced by more advanced forms. Rodents and insectivores took hold. The forerunners of many modern types of herbivores, including horses, rhinos, elephants, deer, and tapirs, first appeared. The carnivores showed little change.

The *Oligocene epoch* ("few recent kinds of life") lasted 13 million years, from 37 million to 24 million years ago. The tropical areas of the Paleocene shrank in size and were replaced by temperate regions. As the epoch continued, forested landscapes were replaced by more savannalike environments. This forced many changes in herbivores, which evolved from tree and bush browsers to grazers.

Horses, rhinos, pigs, tapirs, deer, peccaries, and camels were plentiful in North America. The titanotheres (large rhinolike herbivores with bizarre horns on their snouts) grew to large size but became extinct by mid-Oligocene. The oreodonts (sheep- or piglike animals) formed huge herds, as evidenced by the large numbers of their fossilized remains in the Big Badlands of South Dakota, Nebraska, and Wyoming. The carnivores began to diversify, as the first true dogs, cats (including the first saber-toothed cats), and weasels appeared.

The *Miocene epoch* ("less recent") lasted 19 million years, from 24 million until 5 million years ago. The Miocene was characterized by enormous changes in geography and the resultant intercontinental migrations of animals. Africa moved north against Europe; India collided with Asia, creating the Himalayas; and the Americas moved west against the Pacific plate, pushing up the Sierra Nevadas, Cascades, and other coast ranges as well as the Andes.

In the oceans, sharks, whales, porpoises, and sea cows thrived. Sedimentary deposits in the Atlantic coastal plain are awash with their fossilized remains. On land, the first abundant grasses appeared. A temperate belt existed in the northern United States, and the South was semiarid.

Many mammals had a modern appearance, although most were smaller than present-day forms. In the United States, the fauna appeared much like that of the modern African savanna. Migratory waves of animals moved both in and out of Europe, Asia, Africa, and North America.

The *Pliocene epoch* ("more recent"), the last of the Tertiary epochs, lasted for 3.3 million years, from 5 million until 1.7 million years ago. It was during this epoch, in Africa, that the first hominids began to appear. Continental drift brought most land masses to their present positions. Ice caps forming in the polar regions caused a lowering of both land and sea temperatures. North and South America were now linked, and animals migrated in both directions.

In North America, antelope, horses, camels, deer, peccaries, and gomphotheres (the first elephant stock to reach North America) were abundant. Ground sloths, armadillos, and opossums arrived from South America, and raccoons, dogs, bears, camels, horses, and mastodons migrated southward. In the oceans, sharks, whales, and dolphins were plentiful, as were most modern salt- and freshwater fish.

Tertiary period outcrops are plentiful in eastern coastal regions, from Maryland south to Florida and west to Texas. Outcrops are also abundant from Texas north to Canada and in many places along the West Coast.

Quaternary Period

The *Quaternary period* began with the *Pleistocene epoch* ("most recent") 1.7 million years ago. The Pleistocene, commonly known as the Ice Age, lasted nearly 1.7 million years until about 10,000 years ago, when the *Holocene epoch*, or modern "Recent" time, began (at least for geologic purposes).

In fact, the Ice Age was really a series of ice ages, during which glaciers advanced and then retreated across most of the Northern and Southern Hemispheres. Sea levels dropped by hundreds of feet because ocean water was locked in ice. Some coastlines were perhaps 100 miles farther out to sea than they are today.

North American Pleistocene land fauna included mammoths, masto-dons, saber-toothed cats, lions, short-faced bears, dire wolves, camels, horses, and ground sloths. All disappeared from North America by the end of the epoch, by which time many large land mammals had become extinct. It is not known whether this was due to climatic conditions, the development and arrival of modern humans, or other factors.

Two of the best-known Pleistocene vertebrate sites are the Leisey Shell Pit, south of Tampa (about 1.5 million years old), and the Rancho La Brea tar pits in Los Angeles (about 30,000 years old). Unique to the late Pleistocene is the fact that we can actually see what some extinct animals looked like. Cave art from Europe provides renderings of these animals as far back as 40,000 years ago.

Pleistocene outcrops occur throughout much of the United States. Because of their deposition at or near surface level, modern-day construc-tion activity often reveals new sites.

Technically, the fossil record stops with the end of the Pleistocene some 10,000 years ago. But just imagine, 10,000 years from now, a fossil collector may uncover the remains of an animal or plant that was alive today and wonder what our world was like.

Answers to the Most Frequently Asked Questions About Fossils

What is a fossil?

Simply put, a fossil is the preserved remains of a plant or animal, or the evidence of activity of an animal, that lived more than about 10,000 years ago. The word is derived from the Latin *fossilis,* meaning "dug up." The most common fossils are shells, bones, and teeth, because these tend to be the parts of animals that are most resistant to degradation in nature. Soft tissues or soft-bodied animals are rarely preserved.

How are fossils formed?

Generally speaking, in order for an organism or its parts to become fossilized, it must have died, it must have had hard parts, and it must have been buried rapidly in the right kind of sediment. There are many different ways that fossils are formed, but there are three main kinds of fossilization: preservation with little or no change, preservation with change, and evidence of activity.

Preservation with little or no change

No change. Some organisms or parts of organisms are highly resistant to natural decay due to their chemical makeup. This results in fossils that are virtually unaltered from their original state. The calcium carbonate in seashells, the chitin of marine organisms, and the calcium phosphate in teeth and bones are highly resistant to decay. Typically, shells lose their color, whereas teeth and bones gain color due to staining. Perhaps the best example of original preservation of vertebrate material can be seen at Ashfall State Park in Royal, Nebraska, where the skeletons of dozens of Miocene rhinoceroses have been unearthed.

Freezing. This occurs when an animal dies or is trapped, then freezes and is buried before decay or scavengers destroy it. Typically, these fossils are found in Alaska or Siberia and are of mammoths and other animals from the Pleistocene.

Desiccation, or drying. This occurs when an animal dies in a dry environment and the water in its tissues is drawn out before decay or scavenging occurs. This is similar to mummification and usually occurs in caves. Ground sloths preserved in this manner have been found in South America.

Chemical preservation. Peat bogs, tar pits, and oil seeps are excellent sources of fossils that have been chemically preserved. The Rancho La Brea tar pits in California and Big Bone Lick in Kentucky are well-known sites in the United States.

Freezing, desiccation, and chemical preservation are likely to include soft tissues as well as hard parts. However, because of their rarity and inaccessibility, the average collector is unlikely to come across fossils that have been preserved in these manners.

Preservation with change

Permineralization. This process occurs when minerals from groundwater fill in the small empty spaces in bones, shells, or plants. The original structure may be left in place unaltered. The trees of the Petrified Forest in Arizona are perhaps the best examples of this type of preservation.

Replacement, or mineralization. When groundwater and dissolved minerals remove and replace the structural compounds of shell, bone, or plant, replacement, or mineralization, is said to have occurred. In some cases, both permineralization and mineralization occur in the same fossil.

Carbonization. Most living matter contains a large amount of carbon. Often a thin film of carbon, in great detail and in the original outline of the organism, is all that is preserved. Plant material, fish, and insects are frequently preserved in this manner.

Molds and casts. Most molds and casts are from shelled marine organisms, although in a few rare cases, skin impressions of dinosaurs have been found. An *internal mold* is formed when the organism dies, and sediment fills in the shell and hardens. The shell dissolves away, leaving an exact impression of the inside of the shell. This is also called a *steinkern.* An *external mold* is formed when sediment surrounds the outside of the shell. The shell dissolves and a cavity is left. The impression of the outside of the shell is left on the surrounding hardened sediments. A *cast* is formed by the same process as an external mold, except that a second sediment then fills in the cavity so that an impression of the outside surface of the original shell is left on the sediment that filled the cavity. Occasionally, whole body casts or molds have been found, usually where volcanic ash or lava buried the animal.

Amber. Amber is fossilized resin produced by trees. The actual process of fossilization of amber is not fully understood. Amber is generally found without organic inclusions, but in some cases, insects, small animals, mushrooms, flowers, and even feathers have been found inside pieces of amber. Preservation in amber is considered a special type of mold, as the original tissues have decayed.

Evidence of activity

Tracks, trails, and burrows. The unique aspect of these types of fossils is that they come from living, moving animals. The animals that made them may have been looking for something to eat, seeking a mate, or just passing through, but they were alive right then and there. Dinosaur tracks receive the most attention, but other reptiles, amphibians, birds, and even early humans left their footprints in mud or ash that hardened soon after. The term *trail* is usually used for an insect or marine animal path that has been preserved. *Burrow* usually refers to a tunnel used by shellfish, shrimp, or crabs for safety or for hunting for food, although the most famous example of a fossilized burrow is that of the *Daemonelix* or Devil's Corkscrew from Nebraska, which was formed by a burrowing rodent.

Coprolites. Coprolites are fossilized excrement. Both marine animals (primarily sharks, fish, and reptiles) and terrestrial animals (including dinosaurs) left their remains in this manner. The study of coprolites is valuable, as important information about the diet of these animals and their environment can be obtained.

Eggs and nests. These are very rare finds. Dinosaur eggs and nests get most of the press, but bird, turtle, and other reptilian eggs have been found as well.

Gastroliths. The one case where a plain old rock is considered a fossil is if that rock was swallowed by an animal to be used as a grinding stone in its stomach. The only way to tell if a smooth, rounded rock is a true gastrolith is when it is found with other similar rocks in association with an articulated skeleton. Gastroliths, however, are described as having a greasy or silky feel as opposed to polished rocks which are as smooth as glass. Gastroliths are associated with dinosaurs, birds, crocodiles, and plesiosaurs.

Feeding activity. The most common fossils showing feeding activity are shark tooth scratches on whale bones, evidenced by short, thin pairs or triplets of parallel lines. Occasionally, carnivore puncture holes or pieces of broken teeth may be found in bone.

How can you tell if something is a fossil?

Molds and casts are almost always fossils if their weight feels heavier than an equivalent amount of loose surrounding sediment. Also, tapping it with a metal object should produce a characteristic sound something like the clink of a knife hitting china.

Shells can be tricky unless they are from a species known to be extinct or are found in situ—that is, in the actual sediment. Wave and water action can make a loose, recent shell look quite old in a short period of time.

Teeth and bones are likely to be fossils if their weight seems more like that of a rock than of ordinary bones such as steak or rib bones. Again, tapping with a metal object will produce a characteristic clink rather than the more dull thunk of ordinary bone. Some collectors test the object in question by tapping their teeth with it, preferring to trust the feeling produced rather than the sound. Another general rule is that fossil bones tend to crack or break at right angles to the grain, whereas recent bone tends to splinter along the length of the bone. Burning a recent bone with a match usually produces an unpleasant odor similar to burning hair, whereas a fossil bone will produce no such odor, since there is no protein left in the bone.

Fossils do not bend and generally can't be squished. Using these tests first will save you the embarrassment of having your "fossil" bird bone identified as having come from Colonel Sanders rather than the Miocene.

If you are still in doubt, and you belong to a fossil club, just take it to a meeting and ask someone. If you haven't joined a club, take it to the geology department of a local college or university.

Why are fossils different colors?

The color of a fossil has nothing to do with its age. In most cases, the coloration is the result of the agent that preserved the fossil, although some ammonites, nautiloids, baculites, and shells are found with their original mother-of-pearl coating.

Vertebrate fossils are predominantly black, brown, or gray, because the majority of them were exposed to seawater for some period of time before being buried. This coloration or stain was produced by a chemical reaction between seawater and the calcium phosphate in teeth and bones. Recent teeth and bones will also turn the same color after a period of time in seawater. Other colorations come from minerals in groundwater that are deposited after the fossil is buried. Petrified wood from Arizona and Oregon is famous for its amazing palette of colors.

Paleozoic fossils are most commonly black or orange-red. Black is usually a result of carbonization, and orange-red is the result of oxidation or rusting of iron compounds.

Some fossils appear to be made of gold. Unfortunately, it is fool's gold and not the real thing. Iron pyrite or marcasite is the agent of preservation in these cases.

How can you tell how old a fossil is?

The exact age of a fossil cannot be determined. But don't despair, because collectors can estimate how old something is fairly easily.

Before the development of radioactive isotope dating techniques, paleontologists and collectors had to rely on relative dating. Since no absolute time sequences were known, it could only be said that something was older or younger relative to something else based on the assumption that older sediments would be buried under more recent ones. As such, fossils from deeper sediments were considered to be older than fossils from more shallow sediments. In most cases, this was a reasonable assumption, but it did not hold where the earth had been folded or where fossils had weathered out of sediments.

Interestingly, Charles Walcott, an eminent paleontologist of his time, wrote in 1911 that fossils of the Middle Cambrian Burgess Shale were "buried in mud 15–20 million years ago." He was only off by some 500 million years, but it was a state-of-the-art estimate back then.

At present, the most common method of dating fossils and sediments is the potassium-argon method. This procedure measures the decay of radioactive potassium into argon. Since this occurs at a fixed rate, it is possible to measure the amount of argon from a sample, determine the potassium-argon ratio, and then calculate its age (admittedly, a simplistic explanation). This method is believed to be accurate for time periods from 200,000 years ago back to and beyond the origin of the earth 4.5 billion years ago. Lunar rock samples were tested and dated using this method.

Radiocarbon, or carbon 14, testing is another method used, but it is only useful for dating organic material back to about 40,000 years ago. Obviously, there is a gap between the maximum age that can be dated by radiocarbon and the minimum age that can be dated by the potassium-argon method. Other radioactive dating methods have been developed to date material from this 160,000-year window.

None of these methods, however, are available to the collector in the field. If a collector wishes to know a fossil's approximate age, he need only know which formation he is collecting from, as most formations have already been dated. A formation is a widely distributed body of rock that is distinguishable from the layers of rock above and below it by its composition, the fossils it contains, or both. In most cases, this information is easily obtainable through local or regional guides to collecting or from a State Geological Survey.

How do you know that something is extinct?

About 1.75 million living species, ranging from single-celled organisms to the relatively small group of vertebrates, have been formally identified and given scientific names. It is estimated that another 10 to 12 million may exist. Current thinking on the subject holds that 99 percent of all species that ever lived on earth are extinct, yet less than 250,000 fossil species have been described. These mind-boggling numbers indicate that extinction is a rather common occurrence. But how can we be sure that a species is extinct?

We can be certain in most cases because their remains stop appearing in the fossil record at some point, and living specimens have not been caught, seen, or described by anyone. But two examples show that not everything believed extinct is in fact so.

The most famous example is the coelacanth, a lobe-finned fish that first appears in the fossil record in the Devonian. No fossil coelacanths were ever found after the Cretaceous, and it was assumed that they had become extinct like so many other kinds of animals at that time. Then in December 1938, a living coelacanth was caught by a fisherman off the coast of South Africa. There certainly aren't many left, as it took fourteen more years for another one to be caught. Since then, underwater photographers have recorded the fish and some of their strange behavior for posterity.

A more recent example occurred in August 1994, as a park ranger in Australia explored a 2,000-foot-deep gorge. He discovered a stand of about forty trees of a kind not seen in the fossil record since the Paleocene and never before seen by humans.

Are there other "extinct" species still to be discovered? It's more than likely, but there probably aren't many. While such things as the Loch Ness monster capture our attention, it would seem that rumors of ground sloths in the Amazon jungle are more likely to pan out. And who knows what lurks in the ocean depths?

What gear do I need?

The gear that is needed, or useful, for collecting fossils is somewhat dependent on the kind of collecting. But in all cases, the gear is low-tech and inexpensive. In fact, the Ziploc bag is considered a great technological advance in the annals of fossil collecting.

First and foremost, you need a hat for protection from the sun. A hardhat is necessary for sites where falling rock is a problem, and safety glasses are good to have for certain types of collecting. In many cases, you will be tramping through or in streams or muddy areas, and most collectors have Wellingtons (below-the-knee boots) or hip waders (generally insulated). Old tennis or athletic shoes are fine for areas of flat collecting or for warm-weather water hazards, but a sturdy pair of boots with good traction is essential for other collecting. Over-the-ankle boots are best, as they will help protect against turned or sprained ankles. Athletic shoes with cleats provide the best traction on land, although they lack the ankle protection of boots. You may want to use a walking stick, depending on the terrain or the condition of your knees. Warm-weather beach and bay collectors should invest in a pair of sport sandals and a pair of knee-high socks when stinging jellyfish are a problem.

Perhaps the most expensive item in a fossil collector's tool kit is a good rock hammer. Usually, one end has a square pounding area, and the other end is a pick or a chisel. Choose the one that's best for the type of collecting you do. The pick is good for softer sediments; the chisel helps in harder, layered sediments. Additional metal tools should include several sizes of masonry or cold chisels, a pry bar, hammers, an ice pick, a trowel, and a sturdy knife.

For carrying your finds, you'll need plenty of recloseable bags. For smaller fossils or ones you want to keep separated, 35-millimeter photographic film canisters work well. Most surface collectors—those who do no digging—use nail aprons, available at most hardware stores, for carrying their finds. If fossils are plentiful, take two and tie the second one on backward. When the first apron is full, simply rotate them, and you can keep on collecting without stopping. A sturdy plastic bucket is the conveyance of choice for larger specimens that are not fragile or for fossils that are wet. You can also turn it upside down and sit on it for lunch or a rest. If you are likely to encounter a big specimen, a backpack is a necessity. With a backpack, you can carry all your tools, wrappings, drink, food, and fossils at the same time.

Always have a small roll of aluminum foil or some newspaper for wrapping up fragile or broken finds. Take along a paintbrush and medium-weight gloves when you may be removing specimens from the surrounding matrix. A screen box is essential to sift through stream sediment. You may also want to carry along an inexpensive camera to record fossils that can't be removed from the surrounding matrix or for recording where special fossils came from.

3

Scientific Classification and Other Jargon

Perhaps the most confusing and frustrating aspect of fossil collecting for beginners is the jargon associated with it. Be it scientific classification, species names, geologic and anatomical terms, or just plain slang, it all seems Greek to many. Actually, it's more Latin, but there is some Greek to it as well.

TAXONOMY

Taxonomy is the theory and practice of classifying organisms. Classification is the process whereby individuals are grouped into a hierarchy of categories, or taxa, which are then assigned names. This system is known as the Linnaean system, named after the Swedish naturalist Carl von Linné (often Latinized as Carolus Linnaeus), who developed it in the late 1750s.

The practical importance of such a system is to facilitate identification, communication, and organization of information about different organisms. This system is invaluable, because one type of animal or plant may have several different common names, which can lead to confusion. For example, mountain lion, puma, cougar, panther, and catamount are all common names for the same animal, whose one scientific name is *Felis concolor.*

Each type of animal or plant is assigned by taxonomists to a hierarchical series of seven major groupings, using either increasingly more or decreasingly less shared characteristics, depending on their point of view. The following illustrates the hierarchical nature of classification:

Mountain lion	Human
Kingdom: Animalia	Kingdom: Animalia
Phylum: Chordata	Phylum: Chordata
Class: Mammalia	Class: Mammalia
Order: Carnivora	Order: Primates
Family: Felidae	Family: Hominidae
Genus: *Felis*	Genus: *Homo*
Species: *concolor*	Species: *sapiens*

The foundation of the Linnaean system is a two-word name, consisting of genus and species, to identify each plant or animal that has ever lived or is currently alive, and for the most part, fossil collectors concern themselves with a specimen's genus and species in terms of identification.

The species is the smallest level of differentiation among distinct groups of organisms, although subspecies are sometimes recognized. An operational definition of a single living species is a population of organisms having the ability to mate with another of its kind and produce fertile offspring. Obviously, this is untestable with fossilized organisms, so paleontologists define a species as a group of similar fossils that show no more variation among themselves than is found within a typical living species. With such an open-ended definition, it should come as no surprise that there can be considerable disagreement among paleontologists, especially when a fragmentary fossil is the basis for determination of a new species.

The levels of genus and higher are more abstract than that of species in that there is no operational definition but more an agreed-upon grouping. In some instances, the prefixes sub-, super-, and infra- are used to describe intermediate levels in the hierarchy.

The two-word name of each species is somewhat akin to human names such as John Doe, except that Doe, John would be the proper order. Using the earlier example, *concolor* is the trivial or specific name and can be thought of as the personal name, while *Felis* is the generic name and can be thought of as the surname. The two names taken together constitute the name for a unique species.

Carrying the example further, *Felis concolor* is placed in the same genus as the bobcat *(Felis rufa)*, the common cat *(Felis catus)*, and even the extinct American lion *(Felis atrox)*. These animals are related to the African lion *(Panthera leo)* and the tiger *(Panthera tigris)*, but more distantly, as indicated by the different genus. All of these animals, and many more, are included in the family Felidae (cats). The genus name is always capitalized, and both the genus and species names are italicized. The name of a species is usually in Latin or is Latinized; Greek is also common. Other languages are sometimes used.

When writing, the proper convention is to use the complete species name, such as *Bison antiquus;* however, when using the same name repeatedly in text, it is common to abbreviate the genus by using just the first letter. Additionally, some species names that are recognized easily are often abbreviated in the same way, such as *T. rex*. If only one organism is assigned to a genus, common convention uses just the genus name, as in the case of the Oligocene saber-toothed cat *Hoplophoneus*. When an individual species is not identifiable or when the entire genus has a common characteristic, convention is to use the abbreviation sp. along with the genus name, such as *Equus* sp. (Pleistocene and Recent horses).

TAPHONOMY

Taphonomy is perhaps the most interesting branch of paleontology. Unfortunately, it is the branch least understood by fossil collectors and is the part they are generally least interested in. Taphonomy is the scientific study of everything that happened to a fossil from the moments just prior to the death of the organism to its burial. It is essentially detective work—a homicide investigation with no witnesses is a perfect analogy.

A homicide investigator must examine all the clues at the crime scene to reconstruct who the victim was, what happened to the victim, and how the victim's body came to rest at that place. In studying taphonomy, a paleontologist must determine what animal the fossil belonged to, how it came to rest where it was found, and what the condition of the fossil tells about the individual, its environment, its death, decomposition, and fossilization.

By way of example, try drawing your own conclusions about the following real fossil finds: Why are the remains of mammoths found at the Hot Springs sinkhole site in South Dakota only those of young adult males? What does an extinct fossil shell with marine worm trails, boring sponge holes, and barnacles on it say about its watery world a million years ago in Florida? How did so many nearly complete fossil skeletons of large and small whales, all oriented in virtually the same direction, come to rest near Fredericksburg, Virginia?

NOMENCLATURE

The naming of a new species is a long, drawn-out process that generally starts with the finding of a fossil that appears different in a significant manner from any previously known species. It may be found by, or brought to, an expert, who then begins the process of comparing this specimen with other, similar fossils. If the expert is convinced that it is different, a paper will be submitted for publication in a scientific journal and reviewed by others. As the paper is being written, a new name will be derived according to standards set out in the International Code for Zoological Nomenclature, in the case of animals, or the International Code for Botanical Nomenclature, in the case of plants.

Most species names are descriptive of some aspect of the plant or animal itself. Some species, however, are named in honor of the discoverer, a distinguished person, or the place or region where it was first found. In other cases, a more general description may be used or a more creative one may be employed. The following are some examples of the various ways species have gotten their names.

Discoverer

Titanis walleri, a 10-foot-tall predatory bird named after its discoverer, Ben Waller.

Tullimonstrum gregarium, the "Tully monster," named after Francis Tully, who first found it.

Person or Place

Equus leidyi, a horse named in honor of Joseph Leidy—regarded as the father of American vertebrate paleontology.

Castoroides leiseyorum, a giant beaver named after the family that owned the mine where its skull was first found.

Hyracodon nebrascensis, an extinct rhinoceros many of which were found in the Badlands of Nebraska.

Alligator mississippiensis, the American alligator commonly found both alive today in the Mississippi River and as a fossil.

Chesapecten jeffersonius, a scallop named for a place and a person: the Chesapeake Bay and Thomas Jefferson.

Kyptoceras amatorum, a giraffelike animal named in honor of all amateur fossil collectors.

Generalized Description

Brontops robustus, a large, bulky titanothere.
Smilodon gracilis, a gracile or slender type of saber-toothed cat.

Mosasaurus maximus, a 40-foot-long terror of the Cretaceous seas.

Teratornis incredibilis, a predatory vulture with a wingspan of 20 feet is incredible.

Creative

Hallucigenia sparsa, a bizarre organism populating the ocean floor that became the famed Burgess Shale in Canada.

Paleoparadoxia weltoni, a Miocene inhabitant of the Pacific shoreline sometimes likened to a walrus, sometimes a hippopotamus.

Balanus tintinnabulum, a "ringing" barnacle? Obviously named by an Edgar Allan Poe enthusiast.

One-of-a-Kind

Fubarichthys copiosus, a common fish whose skull is almost always preserved in a state beyond reconstruction. The first part of the genus name is an acronym for "fouled up beyond all recognition."

REASSIGNMENT TO A DIFFERENT TAXONOMIC GROUP

It would seem reasonable to assume that once an organism is named and placed within a taxonomic grouping, that would be the end of the story, but these matters are not necessarily written in stone. For example, until recently, it was generally accepted that the great white shark, *Carcharodon carcharias,* had descended from the extinct giant white shark previously named *Carcharodon megalodon,* both having first appeared in the Miocene and both assigned to the genus *Carcharodon.* Though the teeth of both are similar (the teeth being virtually all that is fossilized), the teeth of the great white, except for its serrations, are, in fact, nearly identical to those of another extinct shark, the mako, *Isurus hastalis.* As such, the giant white recently has been reassigned to a different genus and renamed *Carcharocles megalodon,* while convention dictates that *Carcharodon carcharias* retain its name, although it is now described as having evolved from *Isurus hastalis.*

More controversy surrounds the giant white, as several nearly identical tooth forms exist, primarily distinguished by whether or not there are side cusps alongside the major portion of the tooth. Traditionally, at least two different species have been named, teeth with no cusps being assigned to *C. megalodon,* and teeth with cusps being assigned to *C. angustidens.* But in fact, many gradations from no cusps to full cusps have been found, suggesting that there may have been only one species with wide variation, or more than one species may have existed, but a line of definition based only on their teeth is indistinct.

In any event, some day, with hard work and a lot of luck, you may have the thrill of seeing your name as part of a new species, knowing that you will be remembered in some small way for all time.

GEOLOGIC AND PALEONTOLOGICAL TERMS

The related sciences of geology and paleontology have spawned a whole host of terms to describe various structures and phenomena. Over time, you will become familiar with many of them, but here are a few of the basics you should know from the start.

Formation. More often than not, when looking for fossils, you will be looking for a certain formation from which to collect. A formation is not a specific structure, per se, but a layer of rock or sediment that is distinguishable by its color and composition from layers above and below it. In some places, it may be only a foot thick, and in others, hundreds of feet. Formations are usually named for the locality in which they are first described. Some of the more well known formations include Green River, Morrison, Pierre Shale, Chadron, and Yorktown. Given that different people worked in different areas, it is not surprising that different names for the same formations occur across regions, and a good deal of effort has been expended in trying to correlate them.

Index fossil. Sometimes a certain type of fossil is found across a wide geographic range but only within a fixed geologic time frame. This fossil is then referred to as an index fossil. Index fossils have been cataloged and studied, and they are helpful in the field in determining which formation you are collecting from.

Types. When a new species is discovered and studied, the person who first describes and names it designates a specimen as the *holotype.* Sometimes a group of like specimens is designated as a type series, with the best specimen being designated as the holotype. The holotype is the standard to which similar finds are then compared. A *paratype* is a specimen that depicts some variation within the new species. In some cases, an organism is found that does not correspond with anything, and a new genus or family is created. In such a case, the new taxon is the *type species* (for a new genus) or the *type genus* (for a new family).

Early, middle, late versus upper, middle, lower. These terms are used to describe certain divisions of geologic time. Because the Cenozoic era is the most recent era, more information is known about it, and its periods are further subdivided into epochs. The Paleozoic and Mesozoic periods are subdivided as well, although the names of their subdivisions are less commonly used by non-specialists. In these cases, two sets of descriptions are used. The terms early, middle, and late refer to a time scale, for example, Early, Middle, or Late Cretaceous time. The terms lower, middle, and upper refer to geologic placement, for example, Lower, Middle, or Upper Cretaceous rocks. So, early = lower, middle = middle, and late = upper. To make matters even more confusing, paleontologists frequently combine the terms. The early late Cretaceous, for example, means the first part of the last part of the Cretaceous Period.

ANATOMICAL TERMS

Although invertebrates do have differentiated body parts, for the most part, fossil collectors are dealing with a nearly complete organism. Vertebrates, on the other hand, are far more complex and have many more body parts, and it is a very rare event when an entire skeleton is found. More often, an individual bone or piece of bone is found. Thus, it is highly recommended that you become familiar with skeletal anatomy. Anatomical terms tend to come from Latin, and it may take some time to become familiar with such terms as astragalus, calcaneus, and zygomatic bones, more commonly known as the ankle, heel, and cheekbones.

Anatomical terms are also used to refer to regions of the body, so you will also come across these paired terms: dorsal and ventral, anterior and posterior, rostral and caudal, and proximal and distal. Since most vertebrates have four legs, *dorsal* refers to an animal's back or top side; *ventral* refers to the belly or bottom side. *Anterior* or *rostral* means the forward portion of the animal, and *posterior* or *caudal* refers to the back end. Most limb bones are perpendicular to the body of the animal, and the term *proximal* refers to the end of the bone that is closest to the body and *distal* to the end that is farthest from the body. For example, the proximal part of the femur fits into the pelvis, and the distal end meets with the proximal tibia and fibula at the knee. Figure 3.1 will help you understand these terms.

There also are special terms to refer to hoofed animals. It would seem easier to just call an animal with hooves even-toed or odd-toed. Instead, *ungulates* are referred to as *artiodactyl* or *perissodactyl*. Try that out at your next social gathering. Interestingly, the number of toes these animals have correlates with a host of other characteristics that follow the same grouping.

Artiodactyls have either two or four toes on each foot and include both Recent and extinct pigs, deer, bison, cattle, camels, giraffes, and hippopotamuses. Artiodactyls are the third-largest order of mammals, after rodents and bats. Two-toed artiodactyls have a leg bone called a *cannon bone,* and all have what is called the *"double pulley"* type of anklebone. True horns and antlers are unique to living artiodactyls, as are stomachs that allow food to be rechewed and redigested, a process known as *rumi-*

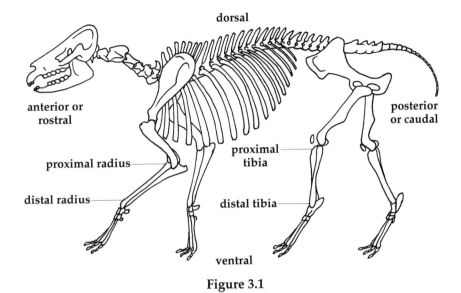

Figure 3.1

nation. However, not all artiodactyls have horns or antlers or ruminant-type stomachs.

Perissodactyls have one or three toes on the hind legs and include the living and fossil horses, rhinoceroses, tapirs, and zebras. Their skulls are long. The nasal bones are elongated and narrow and project forward to points separate from the skull. The eye sockets are always behind the teeth.

SLANG

At a fossil club meeting you may overhear a conversation that goes something like this:

"Hey, I went collecting with a silver pick last week and got some nice stuff."

"Oh yeah? What did you get?"

"I couldn't resist a six-and-a-quarter-inch meggie."

"I went out last week too."

"How'd you do?"

"Just some small fish verts, but mostly PORs and leaverite."

"Too bad."

Translation: The first person, instead of going outdoors to find fossils, went to a fossil show and purchased a very large tooth of the giant white shark, *Carcharocles megalodon.* The second person went outdoors to hunt for fossils and found some small fish vertebrae and some other disappointing items.

Further explanation: Most of what you find when you are fossil collecting can be classified as PORs or leaverite. PORs are plain old rocks and obviously generate no interest from fossil collectors. Leaverite is a mineral that is quite common yet doesn't seem to have made it into textbooks or scientific journals. Leaverite may be found as a POR or it may be found as a common fossil in poor condition. In either case, you might as well just "leave 'er right" where you found it.

Finding Fossils

Learning how to find fossils can be thought of as a three-step process. The first step is to learn what fossils look like. The second step is to locate sites where fossils are present. The third step involves searching at a specific site for fossils.

STEP 1. RECOGNIZING FOSSILS

Many first-time collectors start out by gathering everything that even remotely appears to be a fossil. Later, they try to determine whether any of their finds are, in fact, fossils.

A much better starting point is to learn what fossils look like before you start collecting. Visit as many places as you can that have fossils on display so that you become familiar with them in all their myriad forms. Local guides to fossil-collecting sites usually have an identification section showing potential finds; study them as well.

Appendix A lists the museums, national and state parks, and monuments that have the best collections of fossils available for viewing by the public. Many smaller natural history museums have some fossils on display, and several publications in appendix F list additional outdoor sites maintained by state and federal agencies.

If you are interested in vertebrate fossils, it is highly recommended that you gain an understanding of what whole skeletons and reconstructed animals look like, as well as studying the skeletal anatomy of animals and how their bones fit together. This will be of great value, since you are more likely to find individual pieces of bone rather than entire skeletons. Learn to recognize the characteristic shapes of bones such as the ankle, toe, femur, humerus, and vertebra. Viewing invertebrate specimens will also help you recognize parts of them when you are in the field.

Unfortunately, many museums focus on dinosaur displays and neglect the vast majority of the fossils that you are more likely to find. For this reason, we listed the major fossil shows and exhibitions in appendix B. There are hundreds of other, smaller ones run by local rock, mineral, and fossil clubs. At fossil shows, you have the opportunity to see and hold fossils that you may be able to find in your own region and across the country. Additionally, you will have the opportunity to learn about the dollar value of fossils. Also visit local rock shops and retail stores that sell fossils.

STEP 2. FINDING FOSSIL SITES

Geologists have divided all of earth's rock into three classifications: igneous (melted), metamorphic (changed), and sedimentary (deposited). Most fossils are found in sedimentary rocks such as limestone, shale, sandstone, and mudstone or within unconsolidated (nonhardened) sedimentary deposits. However, some sedimentary rocks and deposits do not contain fossils. So you must narrow your search to fossil-bearing, or fossiliferous, sedimentary deposits.

Maps

The classic way to locate fossil sites involves studying geologic and topographic maps and then using that information to scour the countryside looking for natural outcrops of fossiliferous formations. Without a doubt, this is the most difficult and time-consuming way to find sites, but it appeals to the rugged individualist and can sometimes result in the discovery of entirely new localities. Generally speaking, this method is more appropriate for experienced collectors.

Exposures

You can often find fossils at both natural and man-made exposures. Natural exposures of potentially fossiliferous deposits include river and creek beds, cliffs, mountains, and ocean or lake beaches. Man-made exposures include limestone or shale quarries, coal mines, and sand and gravel pits, as well as their associated waste or spoil piles. Because of liability concerns, it is unlikely that operators of such places will allow you to walk right in, so be sure to check with them first. Road cuts, railroad cuts, and new construction sites may prove rewarding, too.

Published Guides

An easier way to find fossil sites is to use a published guide. Inquire at your State Geological Survey as to whether there are any local guides to fossil collecting. Many of them do publish such information. Several publications listed in appendix F describe various sites where fossils can be found. A word of caution, though—sites may be opened or closed for various reasons, so it's best to check ahead.

Fossil Clubs

Fortunately, there's an even easier way to find fossil sites, and it's not even a secret passed down from one generation to the next. Quite simply, the easiest way to find and collect fossils is to join a fossil club and go on a field trip.

Major fossil clubs located in the United States are listed in appendix C. Most of them are well organized, have hundreds of members, and have regular programs. If you are not close to one of them, there are many smaller clubs. The best way to locate smaller clubs is by contacting the State Geological Survey or the geology department of a local college or university. If all else fails, inquire at local rock or mineral clubs, as their members are likely to have an interest in fossils as well.

Fossil collecting for some is a solitary hobby. That is unfortunate, because there is so much more enjoyment in meeting new people, sharing your finds, discussing current theories, and finding out about those special sites where the field trips don't go. The majority of fossil enthusiasts are only too happy to help out neophytes, and you might make some new friends.

Public-Access Sites

Appendix D lists twelve public-access sites across the country that are some of our favorites. These sites are well known both locally and nationally. They have been open for a long time, they are heavily collected, and yet they continue to produce astounding finds. Treat them gently, please.

STEP 3. FINDING FOSSILS

In general, you should arrive early, stay late, and come back often. You may find a beauty your first time out, but the great fossil hunters come back often enough to remember individual rocks that they have investigated before.

At some sites, fossils are so numerous that you may literally walk over them. And every once in a while, Mother Nature does you a big favor and leaves a prize find just sitting and waiting for you in plain view. But if it was always that easy, this hobby would not offer much excitement.

In most cases, you're going to have to earn that find of a lifetime. More often than not, only a fraction of it will be showing, waiting for the sharp-eyed collector who has prepared mentally before arriving and then uses legs, eyes, terrain, and special clues to find it.

Using Your Legs

When you arrive at a site, rather than wandering aimlessly, you should decide on how you are going to walk it. Over time, collectors develop search patterns that work the best for them. Some search the same way wherever they are, while others may use different patterns at different types of sites. Consider employing some of the more efficient patterns, as follows:

•First, search a site quickly, looking for any large or obvious specimens, then return for more detailed scrutiny.

•Pick a spot at which to begin, and then search methodically until the entire site is covered. (This can feel overwhelming to some.)

•In your mind, divide a site into sections, and then search each parcel until the site is covered. It will feel less overwhelming if you search discrete portions.

•Search an area from at least two directions or at two different times of the day so that shadows fall at different angles.

If you walk upright you are bound to miss some good finds, but on the other hand, if you spend your time on your hands and knees, you won't get very far. A good solution is to mix walking upright with walking bent over. If you do find a pocket or concentration of fossils, then you can get down on hands and knees to search methodically.

Using Your Eyes

Try to keep a mental image of the fossils you are likely to find as you search a site. At the same time, scan for colors, shapes, and textures.

Fossils are frequently a different color than the background material or matrix. Investigate anything that stands out due to its color, such as the black of fossilized bones or the red-orange rust on some Paleozoic fossils. Color is important in the matrix as well. Different coloration of matrices may indicate different formations and thus the right and wrong places to search.

Teeth and bones have characteristic shapes. Investigate anything that has angles or curves that don't match the matrix. For example, shark teeth generally have a triangular shape; the ends of limb bones tend to be rounded or curved.

Also look for textures that don't match the matrix. Bone is usually smooth on its surface but looks like a sponge when broken open to reveal its inside. Look for regularity or repetition when they are not present in the matrix; this could indicate a fossil, such as the ribbing of a shell, the segments of a trilobite, or teeth in a jaw. Again, different textures and compositions of matrices may indicate the right and wrong formations to search.

With experience, you will discover that the best finds tend to come from the periphery of your field of vision rather than the central part. Try to keep the sun to your side or in front of you; otherwise, it will cast your shadow where you are looking. Wearing a hat with a long bill will shield your eyes from the sun if you walk toward it.

Using the Terrain

Some fossil sites are purely flat, and the terrain is not a concern or a help. But more often than not, a site will include hills, valleys, cliff faces, and other features. Inspect the debris at the bottom of walls, cliffs, and cuts before climbing higher. Concentrations of fossils are frequently found where two different layers meet. Also, be sure to investigate any anthills or small burrows at a site; you'll be surprised at some of the small prizes Nature's own earth movers dig up for you.

Gently sloping faces are preferable to vertical faces. A sloping face exposes more of each layer, thus giving you a better chance of finding fossils where present. Also, such a face is easier to climb, and rock is less likely to fall on you.

Collecting after heavy rains and bad storms is usually more productive than during periods of calm weather. Carefully search areas of recent erosion, as they are likely to contain finds that were not visible to previous collectors.

The harder it is to reach a site or a part of a site, the fewer the people that have explored it, and the better the finds may be. But it is imperative that you know your own physical and emotional limits.

Using Special Clues

As you become familiar with a site, you may try looking for more specialized fossil indicators. Sometimes nonfossiliferous material is a clue to the location of fossils. At phosphate mine spoil piles, look for areas with black, pea-size and smaller phosphate nodules. Sediment with large nodules is usually devoid of fossils.

In some cases, certain common fossils are indicative of uncommon fossils. In the mid-Atlantic coastal plain, the scallop *Placopecten* is associated with large shark teeth, and the gastropod *Ecphora* is associated with rare seal and more common porpoise material. In other cases, certain fossils may indicate a lack of other kinds of fossils. Typically, the presence of coral will indicate a lack of vertebrate fossils, although invertebrates may be plentiful.

If you visit a site several times, you may want to try looking for the unexpected. If you are at "Shark Tooth City," change your mental image to mammalian molars, or try scanning for starfish if you are at "Trilobite Town." You won't find many in either case, but you will be doubly rewarded if you achieve success.

DIGGING FOR DINOSAURS: A SPECIAL NOTE

The first dinosaur skeleton found in America was actually unearthed on a farm in Haddonfield, New Jersey. But in general, dinosaurs had an annoying habit of dying and becoming fossils on what is now federal land. What this means for the majority of collectors is that they are probably not going to find dinosaur fossils, because amateur collecting on federal land is illegal. If you contract dinosaur fever, and viewing them in museums does not improve your condition, there is a remedy. Appendix E lists organizations that conduct supervised dinosaur digs. (Inclusion in this list should not be construed as an endorsement, however.) These digs allow you to get out in the field and commune with the "big boys," but there are two drawbacks. First, it's going to cost you—in some cases, a lot. Second, you can take home all the pictures you want, but you don't get to take home what you find or what you work on.

Someday you may actually find a dinosaur tooth or a complete dinosaur bone on your own, but if you do, don't bother playing the lottery anymore; you will have used up your good luck for this lifetime.

A FINAL THOUGHT

Fossil collecting is as much an art as a science, and it's as much hard work as it is luck. In the end, it's the enjoyment you get out of your efforts that determines how successful you are at fossil collecting. But who knows, you may become one of those special people whose desire, enthusiasm, love, and knowledge of fossils create a special sense that cannot be explained and allow you to find what no one else can.

During a softball game in the spring of 1979, I accidentally collided with a teammate. I spent three weeks in the hospital with a compound fracture in my right leg and almost lost it due to infection. Eventually I was able to leave but wore a cast on the entire length of my leg.

The first month home I was in pain and bored. I wanted to hunt fossils, but the doctor wouldn't let me. I began to feel sorry for myself and became bitter for a while. I frequented the fossil room in my house and found some degree of comfort, strength, and peace there.

Another month passed, and I was still wearing a complete leg cast with stainless steel pins sticking out. I couldn't stand being confined to the house any longer, so I decided that if I couldn't hunt fossils, I would at least get near them. Climbing into my car, which luckily had an automatic transmission, I swung my right leg, with the full cast, across the front seat, used my left foot on the brake pedal and a crutch to operate the gas pedal, and headed for the phosphate mines of Florida's famed Bone Valley.

Before the accident, I had spent a lot of time in one particular mine, named Tiger Bay, unearthing prehistoric sea cows and dolphins for the Smithsonian Institution. I loved it because of its unique color combination of green and orange clays and pebbles. The mine also produced fossil elephant teeth of beautiful orange and black hues.

Even if I couldn't climb the tall spoil piles, I could look at them. So for several months and several leg casts, I drove alone and parked my car in virtually the same spot in the mine. I stared out of the open car window at the beautiful orange mountains of spoils across the water.

Eventually, I needed more. I needed the feel of earth under my feet and wondrous fossils in my hands. I've often described the feeling as needing a "fossil fix." Just sitting in my car no longer satisfied me, so one day I got out and crutched around to sample the green and orange clays that lay splattered around. I found several three-toed horse teeth, and I felt alive again. The teeth came out of a gritty orange clay that was overlapped by a slick, smooth green clay. With the help of a pair of binoculars, I could see that the same orange clay was covering the top of the largest spoil pile in the mine, about 100 yards away across the water.

I returned home to determine exactly what species of horse teeth I had found, because horse teeth are index fossils in Florida. I then correlated the species with a specific length of geologic time that had produced a highly fossiliferous formation. I had a feeling that the gritty orange spoil pile might be a haven for a special find. The adrenaline was now pumping; leg cast or not, I was ready for adventure. The very next day I gathered up my courage and headed for Tiger Bay with an inflatable raft, a backpack, and a small army trenching tool.

When I arrived, I used a dive tank full of compressed air to inflate the raft, put my crutches and backpack in, and slipped the raft into the water, somehow managing to get in without capsizing. With my life preserver and cast, I must have made quite a sight.

As I paddled across the water with the trenching tool, I could see the colors of the great hill gleaming in a beautiful early-morning Bone Valley sunrise, the silence punctuated only by the occasional calls of the herons, ibis, and other birds that inhabited the area.

I knew that once I reached the shoreline, getting out of the raft was going to be tricky, not only because of my cast, but also because the footing would be soft and slick. I decided that I would have to roll sideways over the top of the raft onto the shore. I managed to secure the raft with a large rock that, thankfully, was close by, and I rolled away with my crutches and backpack to more solid footing.

As I slowly crutched up the hill, I began to see patches of the slick green clay that had probably lain beneath the orange grit before it had been dug up by the mining operation. Farther up, I began to see large amounts of the orange grit, which was laden with small fossil bone fragments and shark teeth.

Several hours had passed since I had left the security of my car, and the day had become very hot and humid. As I reached the summit of the hill, nearly 80 feet above the water, I was rewarded with a sight even more amazing than anything I had hoped for. In front of me was a 3-foot-long curved horn with an orbit (eye socket) just below it. I fell to my one good knee and was enveloped in a euphoria of achievement and joy.

The surrounding matrix was quite loose, so I brushed it away and gently pulled on the horn to lift it. As I pulled, a partial skull and upper jaw with teeth came with it. The rush of a great high was overwhelming; I had my "fossil fix."

I knew that no living animal looked like this and was certain that no fossil like this had ever been found. I was privileged to be the first human to lay eyes on this magnificent creature. The feelings I had are hard to describe. It was like opening King Tut's tomb or being the first to break the four-minute mile. This is the kind of reward that awaits people who dedicate their lives to a cause. In my case, it happened to be fossils and the search for understanding of our place in time. I had just pulled back the cloak of mystery a bit more.

I spent five more hours on the hill, methodically searching and sifting for more pieces of the animal's skull, teeth, and bones. My effort paid off as I found its other horns, more skull material, and other Miocene and Pliocene fossils.

Shortly thereafter, I took these magnificent fossils to Dr. S. David Webb at the University of Florida. After careful study, he determined that this was an animal previously unknown to science. It was the last species in a line of protoceratids, primitive giraffelike animals that lived 5 to 6 million years ago. The name given by Dr. Webb to this new species was more than generous and appropriate for those who love and cherish the earth as I do. He named it *Kyptoceras amatorum*: *kypto,* Greek for "bent"; *ceras,* Greek for "horn"; and *amatorum,* Latin for "amateurs" and intended to honor all amateur fossil collectors. Interestingly, the Latin root for amateur means "one who loves."

Several months after the initial discovery, I returned to the mine only to find that the hill had been leveled and the material used for other purposes. It was gone forever, and to this day, no other skull material of *Kyptoceras amatorum* has been found anywhere in the world.

You may be lucky enough to make a great find on your first day collecting—it happens. But luck will take you only so far. If you want to make great finds again and again, it takes preparation, knowledge, experience, and most of all, desire and love of what you do.

—F. G.

Diving and Snorkeling
for Fossils

Imagine being in a real-life adventure movie where you are the star. Picture yourself underwater in scuba gear searching for treasures of long ago, perhaps finding an old Spanish bottle, a 10,000-year-old Indian spear point, or a 20-pound molar from an Ice Age mammoth.

See yourself underwater in a river, peacefully gliding past fallen trees as you come upon an alligator resting between the branches. Or perhaps you are offshore in the Gulf of Mexico, hovering above a prehistoric sea cow skeleton while a school of barracuda or a shark investigates what you have found.

Feel the force of a current so strong you must wear 70 pounds of lead on your weight belt. With one hand, you clutch 20 pounds of fossils in your goody bag; with the other, you stab at the riverbottom with a dive knife to keep from being swept downstream.

This kind of fossil collecting is not for everyone, but for those with the experience, physical condition, and emotional capability, there is no greater thrill.

BACKGROUND

For more than two hundred years, paleontologists and amateur fossil collectors have scoured the land looking for natural and man-made exposures where fossils could be collected. In the late 1950s, it occurred to some that there might be another place to look, another environment altogether.

40

Beachcombing along oceans and bays and screenwashing for fossils in shallow streams had always been productive methods for collecting. Why wouldn't snorkeling and scuba diving along coasts and in rivers be productive as well?

In fact, underwater collecting has turned out to be very rewarding and is becoming more popular as the number of land sites and their productivity decline. From the Chesapeake Bay in Maryland south to the coasts, rivers, sinkholes, and underwater caves of Florida, spectacular finds of Eocene through Pleistocene marine and land animals have been made.

How did the fossils come to rest there? In some cases, they had eroded out of formations that are now underwater. In other cases, animals were attracted to freshwater sources and may have fallen in, gotten stuck, or been attacked by predators. After their death, sediment covered their bodies and the process of fossilization began to occur.

Not only are prize fossils such as large shark teeth frequent finds, but so are the remains of land animals such as mammoths, mastodons, giant ground sloths, and carnivores. On occasion, complete or nearly complete skeletons of animals have been recovered.

GETTING STARTED

The best way to get started is by getting your feet wet, both literally and figuratively. Begin by snorkeling in shallow water; it's inexpensive, fun, and relatively safe. If a problem develops, all you need to do is stand up. You are just as likely to make good finds in shallow water as in deeper water, and for most collectors, shallow-water snorkeling is as far as they ever go.

There are some who feel the call of more adventure, however, and decide that deep-water collecting is for them. In order to scuba dive safely, it is essential that you complete a full course in scuba and receive your dive card. Most dive shops will not sell you air without a card. In areas where diving for fossils is popular, most dive shops can give you the names of individuals or groups who share your interest. Remember, never dive alone!

Underwater collecting is not for everyone, but for those who feel the irresistible pull of finding fossils in another world, it presents a unique set of conditions, safety considerations, equipment needs, and collecting strategies.

CONDITIONS

There are several factors that will affect your underwater collecting experience. The first is the clarity of the water. In some places, it is always clear, tannin-stained, or cloudy. In others, conditions may change depending on the season or recent rainfall. For all but the most experienced divers, it is best to avoid cloudy water, even when using a high-powered underwater lantern.

The second factor is the speed of the water current. Unless you are a strong swimmer, it's best to explore where the current is slow.

A third factor is the composition of the bottom material. Fossils tend to stand out better in gravel than in silt, so the collecting will be less time-consuming, although sometimes the faint outline of a fossil may be apparent in silt. In general, hunting in silt is more time-consuming but more productive, since the fossils are not readily apparent and may have been missed by collectors who were there before you. Typically, a riverbottom changes from silt to gravel at different places along its course, so you may be able to try your hand in both circumstances.

SAFETY CONSIDERATIONS

Safety considerations fall into three categories: human carelessness, encounters with animals, and water hazards.

The Human Factor

The first safety rule of diving, whether for fossils or just for fun, is *never go alone.* It only makes sense, but common sense is sometimes not so common.

Second, always remember to watch your air. It is very easy to get caught up in the excitement and find yourself 40 feet down with no air in your tank.

Finally, it is easy to get disoriented in cloudy water. Remain calm and watch where your air bubbles go. Don't allow panic to set in.

Animal Encounters

Animals you potentially will be exposed to may be predatory, poisonous, aggressive, or just highly irritating. When diving in ocean or bay water, sharks are a big concern, but most sharks will not bother you. Great white, tiger, and bull sharks are most frequently implicated in near-shore attacks on humans. Interestingly, more swimmers are attacked by bluefish than by sharks, although the encounter is usually not lethal.

Experienced ocean divers are more concerned about barracuda attacks. Barracuda are attracted to, and readily attack, anything that looks like the small, silvery fish that are their natural prey. Be sure to remove any shiny objects such as rings, metal watches, and other jewelry items before diving where barracuda are present.

Freshwater divers in the southern part of the country don't have to worry about being eaten by sharks. They only have alligators to contend with. There are two schools of thought on alligator behavior. One holds that all alligators are dangerous under all conditions. The other believes that they are dangerous only during breeding season or when a mother is with her young. Numerous supposedly true accounts of run-ins with "logs with legs" suggest that they are not always dangerous. Nevertheless, caution should be exercised at all times.

Experienced freshwater divers are far more concerned with poisonous snakes, particularly water moccasins, also known as cottonmouths. Not only do these snakes swim, but they also tend to rest in tree branches that overhang water. Most people assume that if they see a snake in the water it must be a water moccasin. This is not the case, but rather than trying to identify what kind of snake you have encountered in the water, it's best to give them all a wide berth.

Snapping turtles are another potential safety concern, both in and around fresh water. You won't die from a bite by a snapper, but you may no longer be able to count to twenty on your fingers and toes after a nasty encounter with one of them. Snappers come in two varieties: the snapping turtle and the alligator snapping turtle. The alligator snapping turtle is the larger of the two, reaching up to 4 feet in length and 200 pounds in weight. It can be recognized by its size and the three prominent, knobby ridges along the length of its shell. It is the slower and less aggressive of the two, but it will bite in the water. The snapping turtle is more aggressive, but it rarely bites while in the water. It can be recognized by the three saw-toothed ridges on the top of its tail.

If you manage to avoid running into any of these creatures, you may still encounter floating fire ants. Their bites are not lethal or poisonous, but they are highly painful and irritating.

Water Hazards

In places where the water is fast moving and strong, exhaustion, as a result of constantly working against the current, can be a problem. Some divers tie a rope to a tree along the bank and hold on to it to help slow the effect of the current. Another solution is to stab your dive knife into the riverbottom to hold you. The speed of the current is fairly easy to gauge by observing surface debris floating downstream.

Siphons are downdrafting currents that flow into underground rivers or caverns. Their power can be overwhelming. On the surface, debris that is circling indicates a siphon, but in the water, there is no obvious sign that you are approaching one, so be sure to survey where you plan to dive before going in the water.

Hypothermia can be a serious problem and can occur in cold or seemingly warm water. Immersion in 75-degree water is just as potentially dangerous to a 98.6-degree body as is exposure to 50-degree water. It just takes longer for its effect in warmer water. Shivering is your sign to come out of the water and warm up.

EQUIPMENT

As in fossil collecting on land, equipment for underwater collecting is low-tech and inexpensive except for proper scuba gear. If at this point you are wondering what proper scuba gear is, you should consider remaining an armchair diver until you become certified.

Aside from scuba gear, all you truly need is a goody bag, a nylon mesh bag that can be tied off to hold the marvelous treasures you find. Beyond that, a homemade, 2-foot-long, T-shaped steel bar is very useful for probing into silty bottom material. A table tennis paddle can be helpful for fanning away silt from a likely spot or should you hit something with the probe.

COLLECTING STRATEGIES

In clear, shallow water (less than 2 feet deep), you may actually be able to see fossils while you're wading. Another strategy is to sit on the bottom facing the current and fan the bottom material with your hand to see what's below the top layer of silt.

Snorkeling is the best approach in water that's 2 to 3 feet deep and reasonably clear. Face upstream in a prone position and get as close to the bottom as possible. Hold onto a nearby rock or stab your dive knife into the bottom to hold you in place. With your free hand, continuously wave from left to right just above the silt; with experience, you will be able to determine how powerful a stroke is needed. The current will "blow" the silt downstream underneath you. A pothole will develop below your waving hand, and you will be able to see if any fossils are there.

Scuba gear is necessary in water that is 3 feet deep or more. In some rivers, you may have to dive as much as 40 feet to get to the bottom. Since there is a limited amount of air in your tank, snorkel first to explore areas that seem promising, thereby saving the air in your tank for when you need it most. Again, it's best to stay with clear-water sites.

Just as on land, it is important to use the geography and terrain to help find fossils. The best indicator of a fossiliferous area is the presence of small, rounded, black phosphate gravel. Not all rivers course through phosphate-laden sediments, however.

Any place that can act as a backstop is a likely site for fossils. This includes bends in a river, fallen trees or logs, and accumulations of soft-ball- to boulder-size rocks. Shallow depressions or deeper pits also tend to be accumulation sites. As the river current moves fossils downstream, they drop out of the current and remain there.

Also carefully investigate areas below high, rocky cliffs. The first Americans used high cliffs along waterways to watch for animals coming to drink or cross. At places such as these, the animals were easy targets for spear-throwing hunters 10,000 to 15,000 years ago.

My first official scuba dive for fossils was one I will never forget, mainly because it was almost my only dive.

I joined a group that was headed for the Santa Fe River in northern Florida. I had been certified and had all of the necessary gear for safe diving. Each of us had two tanks of air, 25 pounds of lead on a weight belt, food, drinks, and a bucket to carry back the fossils. The part of the river that we planned to dive had public access, but we had to hike nearly a mile to reach it. I put one tank on my back and the weight belt around my waist, then I balanced the second tank on my shoulder, grabbed my bucket, and started hiking with the group.

When we finally reached the water, I gazed up and down the serene yet eerie river, its banks lined with tall cypress trees draped with long, flowing beards of Spanish moss. I felt one with nature.

We made final preparations on the bank and then slithered into the water. Fish swam around me, oblivious to my intrusion into their dark realm. I slowly descended the 35 feet to the riverbottom and immediately saw a pile of bones that stretched nearly the entire width of the river. I systematically looked and fanned my way across, searching for the better pieces and placing them in my goody bag.

After about an hour on the bottom, I was laboring hard to suck the last of the air out of my tank before I hit the reserve switch, which would give me enough air to reach the surface. When I could suck no more air out, I reached behind my head to flip the reserve switch, only to realize that it was already open. I was 35 feet down with no air left.

Natural instinct told me to drop everything and head for the surface. Fortunately, my brain took control. Shooting straight up would probably have meant death, as my lungs would have ruptured due to an air embolism. I had to act fast, but I had to survive. In a situation like this, you must control your emotions. I knew I had to get to the surface, but I also knew that I must rise no more quickly than my air bubbles. I focused on what I had to do and resisted panicking. Since there was no air left in my tank, I slowly expelled small amounts of the last breath that was in my lungs and followed the air bubbles to the surface.

It seemed like forever, but I finally made it to the top. Gagging and choking for air, I pulled my emergency life jacket CO_2 cartridge and made it to shore. I sat on the bank and retraced every step of the way, trying to figure out what had gone wrong. Then I realized that when I swung the second tank to my shoulder, it must have flipped open the reserve switch on the first tank. I was relieved to learn that it had been a freak accident.

I was also relieved to learn that I wasn't going to have to go back in the water to retrieve the fossils I had collected. Without thinking, I had managed to hold on to my goody bag throughout the entire harrowing incident.

—F. G.

Basic Fossil Techniques

For the most part, fossil collecting is no more involved than picking up a fossil, putting it in your pocket, and driving back home. But there comes a time when some technique for uncovering and determining the size, stabilizing, extracting, protecting and transporting, or repairing a fossil will be necessary. Many of these techniques go beyond the scope of this book; two of the best resources on the subject are listed in appendix F.

UNCOVERING THE FOSSIL
If you find a partially exposed fossil, you must determine the size of the unseen portion. Sometimes, what you see is all there is; at other times, there is more than what meets the eye. In any case, do not attempt to pull the fossil out of the surrounding matrix.

If the matrix is unconsolidated, such as a spoil pile, gently scoop the material away with your hand until you are sure of the extent of the fossil. If the matrix is moderately hard, as in a badland type of environment, use a knife to gently probe around the fossil to determine its horizontal dimensions. At a site where the matrix is hard, it is not possible to do this, but most Paleozoic fossils are not more than several inches long or deep. It is very helpful if you learn beforehand what fossils you are likely to find and their normal sizes and shapes.

STABILIZING THE FOSSIL
Though fossils may have survived millions of years being buried, some are remarkably fragile. Once you have determined the size of the fossil,

you may need to stabilize it. This will help protect it against crumbling or breaking during extraction and transportation.

Butvar (Butvar-76, polyvinyl butyral) is a compound used by experienced collectors as a stabilizer in the field and, in a more dilute solution, as a strengthener at home or in the lab. It comes as a powder that can be mixed in various amounts of acetone to produce the concentrated stabilizer or the more dilute strengthener. It's wise to do this before heading out to collect. Always add the powder to the acetone and work in a well-ventilated room.

Butvar is painted on the surface of a vertebrate fossil to stabilize it. When dry, Butvar forms a shiny, tough film on the surface and seals it. Later, the film can be carefully peeled away with an X-acto knife or dissolved by painting it with a more dilute solution of Butvar.

Older texts suggest using a mixture of water and white glue to stabilize fossils, but white glue absorbs moisture and will expand and contract, ultimately destroying the fossil. However, dilute white glue and some cyanoacrylates will work on fossils that are wet or damp; Butvar will not.

Some rock shops stock Butvar, or you may be able to obtain it through fossil clubs. Check with fossil club members if no ready source is available.

EXTRACTING THE FOSSIL

If the fossil is in an unconsolidated sediment, use your hand to gently move the matrix away. Once the entire fossil has been isolated, it can then be removed from the hole you've made. Be sure to check for associated fossil material by probing vertically and horizontally once the fossil has been removed.

In a moderately hard matrix, such as a badland type of environment, use a sturdy knife to gently probe into the matrix to determine the horizontal size of the fossil. Once the size is established, use the knife to chip away a trench around the fossil. Leave plenty of room between the trench and the fossil in the event that the fossil is larger below the surface. Make the trench wide enough so that you can probe with the knife to determine the depth of the fossil. These actions will produce an isolated block of matrix containing the fossil; this is called a pedestal. It is at this point that a decision about preparing a plaster jacket is made. When you are certain that the correct depth has been established, begin to chip away below the fossil so that only a narrow pedestal remains to support the block. Cradle the block with one hand, and chip away at the base of the pedestal until the block comes free.

At a hard rock site, it will not be possible to determine the size of a partially exposed fossil. In such cases, it is important to know what you are likely to find beforehand. With that knowledge, a reasonable estimate of the fossil's size can be made. Most Paleozoic invertebrate fossils do not extend more than an inch or two below the surace. A trench surrounding the fossil and a pedestal must be made here as well, but the tools and techniques are somewhat different. To form the trench, use a narrow-bladed cold or masonry chisel and a light hammer. Direct the chisel *away* from the specimen. Forming a square or a rectangular trench will help in the extraction. Along one side of the trench, form a double channel, and then chip away at the matrix to form one wide channel. This will allow you to hold the chisel more horizontally when it's time to break the block free of the pedestal.

When you are satisfied with the trench, now several inches deep, switch to a wide-bladed masonry chisel and a heavy hammer, and direct a solid blow to the base of the pedestal. One or two blows will usually do the trick. The more horizontal the chisel, the less likely you are to see the fossil go flying, but in any event, it's wise to put some cushioning around the work area (a jacket or sweatshirt will do) in the event that the force of the blow sends the fossil airborne.

PROTECTING THE FOSSIL FOR LATER TRANSPORT

The decision to make a plaster jacket is usually based on a combination of factors: the condition, size, and significance of the fossil, and how it will be transported.

The actual construction of a plaster jacket is not that involved, but it does require some preparation before leaving for the field. You'll need toilet paper or paper towels and possibly newspaper; plaster and 3-inch-wide strips of burlap, or prepackaged medical plaster gauze strips; and water. Once the pedestal has been formed, mold wet toilet paper or paper towels around the block to about a $1/4$-inch thickness. This will prevent plaster from adhering to the fossil. A layer or two of newspaper is sometimes placed on top of the wet paper to further ensure that the plaster does not stick to the fossil. Never wrap newspaper directly onto a white or beige fossil; you may wind up with ink on it.

Allow this first layer to dry to the point of just being moist. While it is drying, soak the burlap in water, mix the plaster, and then soak the burlap in the plaster. (Prepackaged medical plaster gauze eliminates several steps, but it is more expensive.) Then lay the plaster-impregnated burlap strips around and on top of the block. Be sure to plaster under the block to prevent it from falling out of the jacket. Allow it time to dry (hunt for other fossils nearby), then chip through what's left of the pedestal, turn the nearly encased block over, and finish the job by molding wet paper into the opening and plastering it as before.

An alternative to this process, which works only for small and moderate-size fossils, is "the lazy man's plaster jacket." Stabilize the fossil and form the pedestal. Crumple up some heavy-duty aluminum foil into a ball and then unwrap it. Leave plenty of crinkles in it; don't smooth it out. Wrap the fossil with paper towels or newspaper to avoid scratches from the foil, and then mold one layer of the foil to the wrapped specimen. Next, loosely wrap several layers of the foil around the specimen. The specimen will be held together by the molded layer and cushioned by the outer layers. For extra protection, wrap duct tape around the foil, and you have the near equivalent of a plaster jacket.

To avoid confusion later, mark the jacket as to the specimen, site, date, and orientation of the fossil in the jacket.

PREPARING AND REPAIRING THE FOSSIL

Many specimens can use a little preparation or repair work to make them more attractive. In most cases, a gentle scrubbing with a toothbrush will help remove soft matrix. A sewing needle or a dental pick can be used to remove harder matrix. Another method involves the use of mild acids or other solutions that will dissolve the matrix but not the fossil.

Don't despair if a fossil breaks after you've collected it or if you find it already in pieces. A little cyanoacrylate glue (superglue) will mend it as good as new. These glues come in different viscosities for different purposes; try several different ones on unimportant fossils to see which works best. In some cases, two-part epoxy will be needed for nonporous surfaces. You can try gluing things together in the field, although that can get messy. Another problem with gluing in the field is that you typically don't study your find as well as when you are at home or in the lab, and you may wind up gluing pieces in the wrong place. Generally speaking, the field is not the place to do prep work.

There will be times when you need a third hand to glue broken pieces together or to support a specimen while preparing it. In such cases, there are three alternatives: a sand box, a sand bag, or modeling clay. Each type of support has its positives and negatives. A sand box is good for working on smaller specimens but can be very messy when using glue or other liquids. A sand bag is most useful when working on larger specimens. Modeling clay is especially good for holding pieces of bone in place for gluing, but it contains oils that may be absorbed by the fossil. Eventually, you will find what works best for you.

A word of advice when gluing pieces of a specimen together: Don't complicate matters by gluing all the pieces at once. Glue two pieces together, wait for the reconstructed piece to set, and then proceed.

You can use a light acrylic spray to add some luster to your finds. This is purely a matter of personal preference. Some collectors feel it gives the fossils added visual appeal, but others prefer the look of the fossils as they were found.

Fossil Preparators

There are people whose livelihood is based on their talent as paleontological restorers, or preparators. Most of them work for large museums, and their work centers around stabilizing and preserving fossils. There are also freelance preparators who offer their services to the public. These men and women are true artists, and they can make a crushed or partial specimen look as if it just came from the animal. The names of these people are generally not advertised, but they can be located by word of mouth. As with all things important, there are three factors to consider: cost, quality, and speed. Generally speaking, you only have your choice of two.

One of the top fossil preparators in the country is Karen Chadwick (P.O. Box 376, Interlachen, FL 32148). When asked by prospective customers what she can do, she replies, "Whatever you want. Give me a crushed skull and I can reconstruct it. Give me a toe bone and I can build the whole animal for you. It's just a matter of what you want versus what it will cost."

Most people who contact Karen have found a special fossil such as a skull, jaw, or skeleton that may be in poor condition and want it to be preserved, repaired, prepared, or mounted for display or sale. "In most cases, customers send me plaster-jacketed fossils in boxes, but recently, I completed work on a 26-foot-long elasmosaur that was delivered in a truck." She offers customers a wide range of options, from merely exposing a find on the surface and leaving it in matrix as its own stand to using a special mount that accentuates a fossil's unique attributes. She will also cast missing pieces or locate actual fossils that match what's missing. She can make a fossil look like it just came out of the ground or just came out of the animal.

Customers frequently ask for her opinion about what will look best or make the specimen more valuable. "I make it a point not to express an opinion about how much restoration to do and what work will make it look better or make it more valuable. It's really a matter of personal taste."

Fossil preparation involves a thorough knowledge of art and science, and Karen has studied both. "As a kid, I was always interested in bones. Their shapes fascinated me, and I wondered about their form and function." She graduated with a degree in sculpture and painting from the Ringling School of Art in Sarasota, Florida, intending to be an artist. She was not particularly interested in fossils, but her roommate was a collector. A fossil dealer visited her roommate, saw some of Karen's artwork, and asked if she would do touch-up work on some of his fossils. The rest is history.

Some of Karen's tips for budding preparators and beginning amateur collectors:

1. Ask for advice or help from experienced collectors and preparators. Learn what you can from them, and then see what works best for you.

2. Test materials and supplies on unimportant fossils first. The only way to learn how to stabilize and prepare fossils is by trial and error.

3. Make sure that the fossil and matrix you will be working on are warm and dry. Adhesives, fillers, and paints do not perform as well on cold or wet material.

4. If you want to become a freelance preparator, you have to love what you do.

Sometimes, Karen says, deadlines for shows or the demands of customers can seem overwhelming, but the thrill and excitement of opening up a plaster jacket and extracting a fossil that no one has ever seen in its entirety make it all worthwhile. Ultimately, completing the project and sharing in the enjoyment with the collector is the final reward.

CURATING AND CATALOGING YOUR FOSSILS

As soon as you collect fossils of the same species from two different sites, you will be faced with a predicament: whether to group the fossils by species or by site. There is no right answer. Over time, you will probably store or display them differently as your collection and tastes change. However, it is important to keep detailed information about your finds, and you should have a system of cataloging your fossils.

Figure 6.1 depicts a blank form used to catalog fossils. It is simple and straightforward, yet it contains all the vital information necessary to identify and describe a fossil. Each fossil should have a unique identifier to cross-reference to a catalog as well. Typically some combination of letters and numbers is used to identify the site, specific location, and individual fossil.

In some cases, permanent ink is used to record the identifier on the fossil itself. This is always done in museum collections. If you do so, choose an inconspicuous place to mark the fossil. Some people feel that permanently marking a fossil detracts from its visual appeal and value. If you feel this way, consider using a pencil to write on the fossil or paint a small patch of white, oil-based enamel paint, wait until it dries, and write on the patch. When the ink is dry, give it a coat of clear nail polish to resist chipping or flaking. Another alternative is to keep the fossil in a small box with the information written on a piece of paper or the box itself.

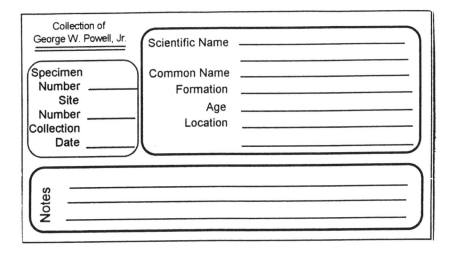

Figure 6.1

In my forty-two years of collecting fossils, I've made more than three thousand plaster jackets. But how could I ever forget my first one?

One day in 1966, I was in a Florida phosphate mine and was knee-deep in water at the bottom of a pit. I was looking up at colorful sequences of neatly layered strata in the cut, or mine wall, methodically scanning for anything that stood out. I caught sight of a small piece of white bone and decided to check it out. I made footholds in the slick clay, pebbles, and sand and slowly made my way up to it.

As I carefully removed the clay matrix from around the bone, a magnificent find was revealed to me. It was the skull of a dolphin—not just any dolphin, but a giant dolphin. Before me was one of the biggest dolphin skulls ever found—nearly 4 feet long!

I quickly made my way back down and ran to my car to gather my plaster-jacketing equipment. I'd never had to use it before, but I was eager to give it a go.

As I headed back to the find, carrying a 50-pound bag of plaster on my shoulder and a 5-gallon bucket loaded with water and tools in my other hand, I heard the ominous sound of a Florida afternoon thunderstorm off in the distance.

I mixed the plaster with the water in the bucket and put wet paper over the specimen, gently molding it to the skull to ensure that the plaster would not stick to the bone. I rehearsed in my mind everything I could remember about plaster jacketing. The specimen was a world-class find, and there could be no mistakes.

Now the plaster was mixed to the right consistency and the paper had set. But wait—I had no burlap cloth to dip in the plaster and make the cast! In the rush of excitement, I had forgotten it. The thunderstorm was now much closer, and I began to panic, as this wonderful find was going to be washed away if I didn't act fast.

They say necessity is the mother of invention, and it's true. I only had one thing with me that I could substitute for burlap. So off came my pants. I used my knife to cut them into 3-inch-wide strips, and within minutes, I was plastering my pants onto that precious skull.

I finished the job and sat down to wait for the plaster to dry when I looked up at the top of the pit wall. Not more than 20 feet away was a mine worker staring down at me. Without thinking, I stood up, then realized that all I had on was my underwear and dry plaster on my hands and arms. The man did a double take, didn't say a word, ran to his truck, and never returned. I stood there imagining the great story he was going to tell someone that day, but I doubt if anyone would have believed him.

After I got home and cleaned up, I thought to myself that I was just crazy about fossil collecting. I bet that mine worker thought I was just plain crazy.

—F. G.

Safety

Fossil collecting is usually a very safe activity that can be enjoyed by the whole family. Unfortunately, injuries and fatalities sometimes do occur. In some cases, they could have been prevented; in others, it was just bad luck. Bad luck can't be avoided, but you can increase the chances of avoiding injuries by educating yourself to the potential hazards that may occur. Hazards can be grouped into the following categories: human behavior, the elements and your body, creepy crawlers, and geography and terrain.

HUMAN BEHAVIOR

Avoid going to deserted sites alone. If you can't go with someone else, at least let someone know where you will be and when you plan to be back.

Always carry a first-aid kit in your vehicle, and learn what to do with it. Also, carry a whistle in case you are injured, and consider pepper spray for the odd animal or human.

Wear brightly colored clothing. If you do get lost or hurt, you will be much easier to locate when wearing something bright than if you wear neutral colors or camouflage. Keep in mind that fossil-collecting sites may also be prime hunting areas, so bright clothing may help avoid an accident.

When arriving at a site, scope it out before getting too far from your vehicle. Look around for fresh footprints or large animal tracks. If something looks suspicious, trust your intuition and leave. It's just not worth the risk.

Know your physical and emotional limits. Most accidents occur because of poor personal judgment, not acts of nature.

THE ELEMENTS AND YOUR BODY

Most collecting is done in warm weather, when the risk of dehydration and heatstroke is high. The most important thing you can do to prevent this potentially lethal situation is to carry plenty of water or sport drink with you *and drink it.* It does no good if it stays in the container.

Mild dehydration symptoms include noticeably yellow urine and mild thirst. Moderate symptoms include noticeable dryness of mucous membranes, dark urine, weak and rapid pulse, and extreme thirst. Severe symptoms include the above plus lack of coordination, drowsiness, disorientation, rapid breathing, pale skin, and no urine output.

It is important to drink *before* getting thirsty and to drink more than what immediately satisfies you. Our thirst sensations are rather poor indicators of our liquid needs. We feel thirsty later than when we should drink, and our thirst feels quenched before we have drunk enough to replace the water we have lost.

When exerting yourself in hot weather, a good habit is to drink and take a short rest every one to two hours, whether you feel as though you need to or not. In the first five to seven minutes of rest, lactic acid buildup in the body is reduced by about 30 percent. In the next fifteen minutes, it is reduced by only about 5 percent more. Thus you don't have to rest a long time to get a meaningful effect.

Some hardy souls like to collect in cold weather. Here, hypothermia is the most common problem. Layered clothing is the best option. Avoid cotton next to the body, as it holds moisture and can bring on hypothermia more quickly than synthetic material. Heat loss occurs most where blood is closest to the skin. Wear a hat and gloves, and keep your feet warm and dry. Consider the first episode of shivering as the last and most important signal to go home.

Always wear a hat. The right hat will keep you cooler on hot days and warmer on cold days, and will sharpen your vision on sunny days.

CREEPY CRAWLERS

There must be something primordial inside us that gives most people the willies when it comes to scorpions, snakes, and spiders. Rationally, we know that most of them are harmless, but a few are potentially lethal. If you don't want to take the time to learn the difference, it's best just to avoid them all. When collecting, always watch where you put your hands.

Scorpions

Scorpions truly fit the description of "living fossils." In one form or another, they have been here for more than 400 million years, and they have not changed very much from the earliest forms.

Scorpions are found throughout the southern half of the continental United States, but only one species is considered potentially lethal. Its range is limited to Arizona, desert portions of California, and southern Nevada. This scorpion, the bark scorpion (*Centruroides sculpturatus*), grows to only about 2 $^1/_2$ inches in length and is greenish yellow or straw colored. It inhabits loose tree bark and rock- and woodpiles. Its sting, unlike that of other scorpions, causes little swelling or inflammation at the sting site. Instead, it produces radiating pain, numbness, epilepticlike seizures, and other cardiovascular and neuromuscular symptoms.

Other species of scorpions can deliver painful or debilitating stings, although most merely produce swelling and irritation at the sting site. A good rule of thumb is that the larger the scorpion and its pincers, the less venomous the sting. So although a big 6-incher may scare the heck out of you, it's the little ones that pack the wallop.

Scorpions are nocturnal hunters and can frequently be found under rocks during the day. When collecting in the Southwest, a good practice is to tuck your pant legs into your hiking boots. Turn over any rocks with a rock hammer by lifting the end farthest away first. This gives a surprised scorpion the opportunity to scurry away rather than run up your pant leg.

Snakes

Snakes are everywhere, although they are rarely seen. Of the hundreds of species that inhabit the United States, nineteen are venomous, including fifteen rattlesnakes, two moccasins, and two coral snakes. Some of these poisonous species are further classified into subspecies, so that almost forty named forms are recognized.

Death as a result of snakebite is infrequent. Most healthy adults may suffer very serious effects, but children and the elderly are far more at risk. The factors that most determine the outcome of a venomous bite are the amount of venom actually delivered and its placement. Even a small amount of venom delivered into a major blood vessel will cause death.

Rattlesnakes are the most numerous of the venomous snakes in the United States, in terms of both species and numbers. They can be found in city suburbs, deserts, mountains, forests, rivers, and swamps. As the name implies, they are best identified by the "rattle" at the end of the tail, although sometimes the rattle is missing. When threatened, most rattlesnakes will coil, face the intruder, hiss, and vibrate their rattles to create a loud, high-pitched warning buzz. Given an opportunity, rattlesnakes will try to escape rather than attack. Most bites occur when people accidentally startle one. The biggest and most lethal of the rattlesnakes is the eastern diamondback, easily recognized by the yellow and dark brown diamond pattern on its back.

The cottonmouth, or water moccasin, and the copperhead are related but inhabit different environments. Young cottonmouths are frequently mistaken for copperheads. As they reach adulthood, cottonmouths loose their copperheadlike pattern and develop a solid black body. Cottonmouths, both young and old, have a dark lateral stripe on the cheek that runs through the eye, with patches of white above and below the stripe.

The cottonmouth seems to have a different temperament than other venomous snakes in that it tends to hold its ground rather than trying to escape. When annoyed, it will vibrate its tail even though it has no rattles, open its mouth to reveal the whitish "cotton" lining, and expose its fangs. It will bite in the water in self-defense. Contrary to popular belief, most snakes encountered in the water are not cottonmouths. One sure way to identify it from others is that cottonmouths swim with their heads well above water. Rattlesnakes and copperheads occasionally swim too. Cottonmouths range from the mid-Atlantic west to the southern plains and south to Texas and Florida.

Copperheads are named for the orange or copper coloration of the head. They can be found in wet or dry areas. Like cottonmouths, they also are easily irritated. The pattern of alternating light and dark brown bands on their backs makes them virtually impossible to discern when coiled in a pile of leaves. Nests of copperhead young have a distinctive odor sometimes likened to the smell of green onion. Copperheads range from southern New England west to Kansas and south to Texas and Georgia.

Two species of coral snakes inhabit the United States. The Arizona coral snake is the smaller of the two. It rarely exceeds 18 inches in length and is restricted primarily to Arizona. The eastern coral snake reaches about 30 inches in length and inhabits parts of the Southeast. It is most commonly found in Florida.

Coral snakes have black noses and a pattern of alternating bands of black, red, and yellow. Two nonvenomous snakes, the scarlet king snake and the scarlet snake, mimic the coral snake's coloring and also overlap in range. The distinguishing characteristic of the coral snake is that the red bands always touch yellow bands and the head is black. The two mimics display red bands touching black bands and have red heads. There are a couple of jingles to help remind you which snakes should be avoided: "Red on yellow, deadly fellow. Red on black, friend of Jack" or "If red is next to yellow, as on a traffic light, stop!"

Coral snakes are shy and almost always try to escape when threatened. They do not coil and rarely strike out. When they do bite, however, they hang on tenaciously and attempt to bite repeatedly.

Current thinking about treatment of venomous bites dispenses with the old cut-and-suction, tight tourniquet methods. Unless venom is delivered directly into a vein or artery, it will take as long as two hours for serious effects to develop. Therefore, the primary emphasis should be on reaching a knowledgeable medical facility quickly rather than immediately delivering first aid. Again, it cannot be stressed too much that you must watch where you put your hands and feet.

Spiders

Nearly thirty thousand species of spiders have been described worldwide. All of them are carnivorous, and all have venom. In the United States, only the tarantula, brown recluse, and black widow spiders have venom that is potentially lethal to humans.

The tarantula is the biggest of the three and certainly the most fearsome looking. As in the case of scorpions, looks can be deceiving. In most cases, the bite of the species inhabiting the United States is no more lethal than a wasp or bee sting. Tarantulas are found in the Southwest, primarily in Arizona. They are docile and spend most of their day in underground burrows.

The brown recluse spider is a small gray, tan, or orange-yellow spider, identified by a dark brown, violin-shaped mark on its cephalothorax. Its venom is highly toxic to humans, with both short-term and longer-lasting effects. Fatalities are very rare. The venom kills cells surrounding the bite and produces a black, gangrenous spot. Often the skin around the bite will peel away, exposing underlying tissue, and will leave an obvious scar when healed. Brown recluse spiders frequent log piles, spoil piles, and clothes piles. They range from Kansas and Missouri south to Texas and west to California.

There are five species of black widow spiders in the United States, but the southern black widow is the most common. The female is shiny black and round and exhibits a red hourglass mark on the underside of the abdomen. The adult female body length rarely exceeds $1/2$ inch.

Ounce for ounce, the venom of the black widow spider is more lethal than snake or scorpion venom. Black widow venom is fifteen times more potent than that of rattlesnakes. Only the female is lethal to humans. The female stays almost exclusively in her web but will bite aggressively at anything that comes close to it.

Symptoms of a black widow bite include extreme pain around the site (which builds to maximum intensity about thirty minutes afterward), nausea, vomiting, faintness and dizziness, salivation, and sweating. Most muscles become rigid, especially in the abdomen. Deaths have occurred as a result of a misdiagnosis of appendicitis. As with snakebites, the emphasis should be on getting the victim to a hospital quickly, where an antitoxin can be administered.

Black widow spiders are frequently found in woodpiles, spoil piles, and portable toilets. They range from Massachusetts south to Florida and west to California.

GEOGRAPHY AND TERRAIN

Safety hazards regarding geography and terrain can generally be divided into two categories: what falls on you and what you fall on (or in).

Collecting along the bases of cliffs and banks can be very dangerous. Keep in mind that the reason fossils are found there is that they fell down. You were lucky enough not to be there when it happened. Sometimes only a small rock comes loose—dangerous enough without a hardhat. At other times, there may be a rock slide or part of the cliff or bank may give way. Never undercut a cliff or bank, as that is likely to re-create the conditions that naturally generate slides and falls.

Always look up and ahead of where you are walking to see if anything is overhanging, and don't linger underneath. If you do hear what sounds like a slide or something giving way above you, your natural instinct is to look up to assess the situation. That is the worst thing to do. Some people will instinctively run forward along the base without looking. That is still not good, although it may reduce your chances of being hit. The best thing to do if you hear something giving way is to resist the urge to look up, and run out and away from the cliff.

Be especially careful walking around pools of water or in streams. There is no way to describe the feeling of walking on firm footing one second, and the next second being up to your knees, waist, or arms or swimming for your life.

A walking stick doesn't have to be anything fancy, but it will help avoid soft areas or unexpected deep holes. It also relieves a lot of the stress on your knees that hiking and climbing generate.

Some sites are relatively flat, and you can spend the day surface collecting with little concern for injury. However, many good sites either require some effort to get to them or are punctuated by hills, valleys, slopes, and other obstacles. The best tips and techniques for successfully and safely navigating terrain like this come from experienced hiking and skiing sources rather than paleontological texts.

Going Up

Unless you are climbing a slope with boulders, and thus have good hand-holds (remember, watch where you put your hands), you should adopt a switchback pattern of ascent. Walk sideways and up along the face of the slope in one direction, then turn and do it in the other direction. Alternate until you reach your objective. It will take you longer to get where you are going, but it is easier on the knees and takes less effort than just going straight up. Climbing in a switchback pattern also places your boots roughly parallel to the slope, thereby placing more surface of the boot in direct contact and lowering the chances of your feet slipping out from under you. If straight up is the only way, use short steps, as this puts less stress on the knees and is less fatiguing.

Coming Down

When descending a steep, rocky slope that provides hand- and footholds, it is best to come back down facing the slope. If you do slip, this position ensures that you won't come down head over heels.

Walking down is a bit different from walking up, in that switchback-ing is less of a benefit. The one thing to avoid, however, is descending a slope with your feet pointed toward the bottom. You will quickly gain speed to the point that you are out of control and may find yourself doing somersaults for a very long distance.

The most important safety factors in descending slopes are speed and the position of your body. First, pick out a line of descent. As you come down, do so slowly. Try not to stop, as you may teeter indecisively. Adopt a skier's stance, with your chin up, knees bent, and arms slightly out and in front. Your center of gravity will then be such that you are reasonably balanced, but if you do slip, you will fall backward, not forward.

Foot position is also important. Try to descend so that your feet are somewhere between parallel and perpendicular to the face of the slope. This position gives the best control.

If your feet and your nerve can't handle walking down, don't be embarrassed to just sit down and slide or scoot. A new pair of jeans might cost $40, but a hospital stay will certainly cost more than that.

This chapter serves merely to point out common and some not-so-obvious hazards. The focus is on prevention, not treatment. In no way should it be taken as the only source of information to rely on. In particular, you should become familiar with information and techniques covered in outdoor safety, first-aid, and survival texts.

After reading this chapter, you may decide never to leave your house for the great outdoors again. But knowledge of potential hazards will help prevent a fun family outing or a marvelous personal adventure from turning into a disaster.

I have been taking groups of amateur fossil collectors to hunt Oligocene fossils in the White River Badlands of Nebraska since 1989. It's a wonderful experience, the fossils are plentiful, and everyone keeps what they find because we are always on private land with the owner's permission. The hunting is particularly good during a rainstorm or soon after, as the water washes away the soft matrix that surrounds the more resistant fossils.

On one rainy day during a trip in 1996, I was having great success finding bones, jaws, and skulls. I came to a 3-foot-deep ravine through which the accumulated rainwater was gushing. In the wall of the ravine, just above the waterline, was a beautifully articulated oreodont skeleton slowly being exposed. I could see the skull, ribs, vertebrae, and legs, all a magnificent dark blue–chocolate brown color.

Now, pieces of oreodonts (sheeplike animals) are the most common fossils in the Badlands, but a complete skeleton is a rare find. I was quickly beginning to plan how I would expose and jacket the find, when I saw that there was a large butte overhanging the oreodont. Immediately, I decided that this was one precious treasure that was going to elude me. It was not worth the risk.

I stayed there for some time, even sat and ate my lunch, watching as the pieces of the skeleton dropped into the rushing water below it. I thought about how that skeleton had lain there for perhaps 35 million years. Then, on this one rainy day, it glimpsed the light of day for a fleeting moment before returning to the arms of Mother Earth.

Not only did I stay to watch this happen, but I also stayed to make sure that none of the trip members developed a bad case of "fossil fever" and tried to retrieve the oreodont from underneath the looming butte.

After the skeleton was completely gone, the overhang was considerably larger and more dangerous, but it had not fallen. In fact, I returned to the same spot two weeks later, and the overhang was still there. I was not disappointed, though, because my decision not to retrieve the oreodont had guaranteed that I would be back.

—F. G.

Laws, Ethics, and Etiquette

LEGAL ISSUES

Most fossil-collecting sites are on property that belongs to a person, a company, a state, or the federal government. In the first two cases, it is important to obtain permission to venture on, and remove fossils from, the property. If it is apparent that the owner lives on the property, visit the residence in person to ask permission. If it is not obvious who the owner is, do some detective work to find out, and ask permission by phone or letter.

There is usually no problem getting onto government land, but amateur and commercial collecting is illegal on federal property, although some states may allow the removal of fossils from certain state-owned sites. The prohibition of collecting on federal land stems from the Antiquities Act of 1906. The reasoning behind the law is that the government has the responsibility to protect antiquities or objects of historical or scientific interest that are the property of all the people. Under the law, permits to excavate and remove items may be issued by various departments or agencies to properly qualified institutions. The law requires that the finds be permanently preserved in public museums.

Additionally, each state may have its own highly specific laws applying to property rights, antiquities, and even the kinds of fossils that may be collected. The following are some examples:

Maryland. Property ownership ends at the high-tide line. This is generally evidenced by the highest accumulation of debris on a beach or bank. Thus, collecting below that line along the Calvert Cliffs or the Maryland side of the Potomac River is not considered trespassing.

Virginia. Individual/personal property ownership ends at the low-tide line, so collecting on the Virginia side of the Potomac and other river sites *is* considered trespassing, unless you are actually in the water below where that line would be—a rather difficult assessment.

Montana. Collecting of fossils is allowed on private land subject to trespass, etc., but it is illegal to transport legally collected vertebrate fossils out of the state.

Florida. Anyone engaging in buying, selling, trading, or systematically collecting vertebrate fossils recovered from state owned, leased, or designated land or rivers must obtain an annual permit from the Florida Museum of Natural History. The permit costs $5, and at the end of the year, the collector must submit a list of fossils found and the localities. Since the fossils are state property, the museum staff may claim scientifically significant ones. If no claim is made by the museum within sixty days of receiving the list, the collector may retain them.

Illinois. In addition to a prohibition against collecting in state parks, preserves, and public land, it is illegal to collect from any sites "known and included in files in the Illinois State Museum," maintained under Illinois statutes.

Alberta, Canada. Canadian citizens may collect and keep any fossils from public land, but they may not be transported out of the province. Foreigners may collect fossils but may not keep them. This essentially makes it useless for foreigners to collect.

Admittedly, the chances of being caught breaking any of these or related laws are quite slim, but there are many sorry tales of arrests and fines from people who were doing the wrong thing in the wrong place at the wrong time.

Consider the case of Sue, the *Tyrannosaurus rex.* Peter Larson, a commercial fossil collector and founder of the Black Hills Institute of Geological Research, Inc., a private earth science fossil and mineral business, frequently collected in South Dakota. Larson and some coworkers were invited by Maurice Williams, a rancher, to look for fossils on some of his land adjacent to the Institute's excavation site in north-central South Dakota.

In August 1990, Susan Hendrickson, a member of Larson's team, discovered some pieces of bone weathering out of a cliff. Larson identified the fragments as having come from a large theropod, possibly a *Tyrannosaurus.* After receiving permission from Williams to excavate at the site, a team from the institute spent fourteen days removing more than 10 tons of bone and matrix. The as-yet-unidentified skeleton, now named Sue, was transported back to the institute, and Williams was paid $5,000 for the right to the excavated skeleton.

After some initial prep work, it was determined that this not only was a *Tyrannosaurus rex*, but it was the largest and most complete specimen of this dinosaur ever collected. Larson publicly announced the discovery and excavation, along with plans to build a museum with Sue as its centerpiece.

That's when the trouble began. The Cheyenne River Sioux claimed ownership of the fossil because it was found within their reservation's boundary. Williams claimed it was his, and that he had accepted the $5,000 from Peter Larson only for permission to search his land, not as payment for something that could be worth $1 million. The federal government also stepped in, claiming that the *T. rex* was its property, since Sue was a national treasure and therefore was covered under the 1906 Antiquities Act, making it illegal to remove her from public lands without government permission.

Then acting U.S. Attorney Kevin Schieffer, using the 1906 Antiquities Act as legal justification, obtained a search warrant on May 13, 1992, to seize Sue and any related fossils and paperwork as evidence for a criminal case against Larson and his colleagues. Government agents and national guardsmen packed and removed the fossils and files, which were then stored in the machine shop at the South Dakota School of Mines and Technology in Rapid City.

Schieffer initially maintained that the warrant was served on the Institute only, and that the seizure of Sue was necessary to prevent Larson from selling this national treasure and to preserve Sue for the people of the United States, since she was the property of the U.S. government. Several months later, when it became obvious that the Antiquities Act did not apply to fossils, the U.S. Attorney's office issued a statement indicating that the seized material would be held as evidence in an ongoing criminal investigation unrelated to the collection of Sue. No criminal charges were ever brought against the Institute or any person for the collection of Sue.

A Federal District Court judge eventually ruled that Sue was real property (real estate), not personal property and not a part of the surface rights of the landowner. Since Williams had put the land from which Sue had been excavated in trust to the U.S. government, he could not legally enter into a contract to sell it without having sought and received written permission of the U.S. secretary of the interior, who acts as trustee for all Indian trust lands. Though this ruling was challenged, the U.S. Supreme Court refused to hear arguments, and the decision stands.

The court's ruling regarding ownership of Sue took on confusing aspects in that when the skeleton was in the ground, it was considered real estate and thus belonged to the U.S. government. Once it had been excavated, it then became the personal property of Williams.

More than eighteen months after the seizure, a grand jury handed down a thirty-nine-count indictment against Larson, his brother, Neal, the Institute, one employee, and two associates, charging theft and retention of government property, conspiracy to steal and sell government property, customs violations, and other acts, all of these unrelated to Sue.

After the longest criminal trial in South Dakota history, a jury acquitted the defendants on most charges, was hung eleven to one for acquittal on others, and convicted on eight felony and five misdemeanor counts. Five of the felony counts were dismissed prior to sentencing. The government chose not to retry on those counts or the counts on which the jury was hung.

Sentencing came in January 1996 and was as follows: The Institute was fined $5,000 and placed on two years' probation, Neal Larson was fined $1,000 and placed on two years' probation, and Peter Larson was sentenced to two years in a federal penitentiary, fined $5,000, and put on two years' probation upon release.

In January 1997, Williams announced plans to auction Sue through Sotheby's Auction House in New York City. On October 4, 1997, Sue was sold for the staggering sum of nearly $8.4 million, far exceeding Sotheby's estimate of a $1 million sale price. The buyer was Chicago's Field Museum of Natural History with the help of substantial corporate sponsorship. It is expected that Sue will be put on display in 2000.

Obviously, this is an extreme case, but it does make the point that you must know what you are doing. The best way to avoid problems is to contact the Geological Survey of the state that you plan to collect in and ask for the local rules, regulations, and statutes. Again, this is another case where joining a fossil club will help. At least some of the members will be knowledgeable about such matters, so don't be shy about asking for help or information.

ETHICS AND ETIQUETTE

By its nature, fossil collecting does not open itself to many cases of ethical problems. Of course, altering or misrepresenting fossils for later scientific investigation or sale is an unequivocal ethical violation.

Some mining companies are enlightened enough to allow collectors and organized groups to collect on their property. It is a privilege and not a right; don't jeopardize others' ability to collect by attempting to seek entrance surreptitiously or by disregarding the rules when allowed on their property.

Unlike ethics, problems involving etiquette do arise frequently. Treat the property of others as if it were your own. If you come across a fence gate that is open, leave it open. If you must open a gate, close it behind you. Carry out your trash. Cover up holes that you have made. Show the owner your finds, and offer to leave him or her one of your nice ones.

Leave some finds for others who follow. It is estimated that a single shark could produce up to twenty thousand teeth in a lifetime; there's no reason to keep every one. If you decide that you don't want to keep some of your specimens, don't throw them out. Donate your expendables for the kids' sand pit at the local fossil show; who knows, you might start the next great paleontologist on a career path.

If you do find something of significance, it does no good sitting in a box in a basement. At the very least, lend it to a museum. It may be hard to do, but donating significant finds to a museum, if asked, is a good practice. You should receive a letter of appreciation, and you will know that you made a contribution to science. In some cases, the museum may make a reproduction or a cast for you. Be sure that your find is indeed something that should be donated for the sake of science, however, rather than just being one of any number of things that a museum would like to add to its collection. Remember, it's your choice.

The Bone Wars
Perhaps the worst example of a breach of ethics and etiquette in the annals of all of science occurred between the two greatest vertebrate fossil hunters in American paleontology: Edward Drinker Cope and Othniel Charles Marsh. These two men started out as friends in the late 1860s but became mortal enemies during a decades-long battle of egos, which ended only with Cope's death in 1897.

Cope was eccentric, married, and lived in Philadelphia. His home and his museum next door served as his base. At various times, he was associated with Haverford College and the University of Pennsylvania. Marsh was a deliberate thinker and a lifelong bachelor. He built a laboratory at Yale University and became part of the academic and political elite. Marsh and Cope, their assistants, and their hired hands combed the Plains collecting many new finds, primarily dinosaurs, in the early 1870s. Their problems began to arise over Cope's describing and naming fossils for which Marsh thought he should be given credit. Their criticism of and hostility toward each other is evidenced both in letters to each other and in scientific journals of the time. Their disdain for each other continued to increase over the years, as each raced west trying to find, describe, and name more new fossils than the other.

In 1882, Marsh was appointed to the post of vertebrate paleontologist of the U.S. Geological Survey. Marsh had become the most famous scientist in America and was well known both by the public and in the halls of Congress.

By the late 1880s, Cope was lagging far behind Marsh in money and prestige. He began to recruit Marsh's assistants to provide negative information about him both personally and professionally. Marsh's poor treatment of his staff ensured that Cope got all the information he wanted.

In 1889, Marsh responded to Cope's attacks by pressuring the secretary of the interior to demand that all of Cope's vertebrate fossils be turned over to the U.S. National Museum, which was controlled by Marsh, on the grounds that they were government property. The claim was untrue, and all parties involved knew it, yet Cope was forced to defend himself.

Cope responded with bitter attacks on Marsh's scientific and personal ethics and abilities. The accusations flew back and forth, spreading to the newspapers through a journalist who recognized that a great story was developing. Eventually, Cope won the war when Congress cut off funding of Marsh's work in 1892 and forced him to resign his post at the Survey.

Subsequently, Cope was able to raise some money and continued to do fieldwork until his death in 1897. Cope's collection of American fossils contained 463 different species. Shortly before his death, he sold it to the American Museum of Natural History in New York for $32,000. Much of the best of his collection had been sold earlier to finance his expeditions and living expenses. Another collection of living species and fossils sold for $29,000.

Marsh had not done serious fieldwork after 1874, preferring to hire people to collect for him. He spent his last years, until his death in 1899, continuing his studies and publishing papers. Marsh's collection included specimens of nearly 450 species and was donated to the Peabody Museum at Yale University. The gift was valued at over $1 million.

Thus ended one of the greatest periods of paleontological discovery in America, unfortunately marred by the bitter rivalry of its two main participants.

ONGOING ISSUES

The case of Sue served to bring to a head the long-standing tug-of-war between amateur and commercial collectors and academics. Some academics have tried to keep commercial and amateur collecting to an absolute minimum. Their aim is to keep important fossil specimens out of the hands of private collectors, thereby ensuring their availability for research and public enjoyment.

Commercial and amateur collectors contend that they serve an important purpose and have a right to search for fossils. Indeed, perhaps tens of millions of dollars worth of fossils have been donated to museums around the world by conscientious amateur and commercial collectors.

This debate has reached the halls of Congress, and in 1996, it resulted in the introduction of two diametrically opposed resolutions, one recommending that fossil collecting by nonacademics be illegal and banning the private ownership of fossils, the other proposing the opening up of federal lands to all fossil collectors with minimal regulatory interference. It seems unlikely that these issues will be resolved anytime soon.

9

Buying and Selling Fossils

It is surprising to many that the buying and selling of fossils and related items is a flourishing business. Since this occurs with works of art, stamps, coins, minerals, antiques, and artifacts, why not fossils?

Perhaps it's difficult to imagine that things with such great scientific value are available for purchase and sale. As mentioned earlier, there are some professional and amateur paleontologists who are vehemently opposed to the personal ownership of fossils, much less a vibrant business in buying and selling. The vast majority of fossils have little scientific value, however, whereas they may have great intrinsic or investment value for a collector.

A distinction is drawn here between a fossil hunter, who searches in the field for fossils, and a fossil collector, who hunts with a silver pick. In many cases they are one and the same, but in some cases they are not. It is the fossil collector who appreciates fossils as something to treasure for their beauty, significance, or investment value. As with other collectibles of value, there are different ways to go about collecting and several factors you should become knowledgeable about.

In general, vertebrate fossils are more highly prized and thus more valuable than invertebrate fossils. First, vertebrate fossils are less common than invertebrates. Second, for some, it is hard to get excited about a crinoid or a trilobite, whereas it is easy to get caught up in the wonder of a 6-inch shark tooth, the skull of a saber-toothed cat, or the giant molar of a woolly mammoth. Sometimes hefty prices may be paid for beautifully prepared or rare fish, plant, insect, or marine invertebrate specimens, but by and large, backboned animal fossils are usually the most expensive and exhibit the greatest potential price appreciation.

Within the vertebrate category, there is a general hierarchy of desirability. Whole skeletons are most highly prized, followed by skulls, jaws, and teeth. Individual bones do not attract much attention unless they come from something big or unusual, exhibit pathology, or show predation by a carnivore.

As with other collectibles, the value of a fossil is determined by such factors as supply and demand, the effort and cost of collecting and preparing a specimen, and even what may be "hot." Shark teeth jumped in price after the release of the movie *Jaws,* and amber did the same after *Jurassic Park.* In the end, the value of a fossil depends on what someone is willing to pay for it. For example, it doesn't cost much to buy some paint and apply it to a piece of canvas. But if the way the paint is applied appeals to someone, the painter may be able to charge an exorbitant price for it totally unrelated to the cost of producing it. Another person may not be willing to pay any price for the same painting. The same is true with fossils. Fossil prices are also affected by general economic conditions. When the economy is good and people have more disposable income, overall prices may rise, and vice versa.

In many ways, fossil prices and values reflect the same forces as other collectibles. However, there are two factors at work in the fossil business that do not reflect trends with other kinds of collectibles. Within the last two decades, the number of fossil collectors has increased, but the number of sites available to collectors has decreased, so there are more people searching at fewer sites. These factors have contributed to dramatically rising fossil prices. Small shark teeth can still be purchased for a nickel, and common trilobites may still be had for a dollar, but tooth, skull, and skeleton prices have skyrocketed.

For example, in the mid-1980s, a 6-inch *Carcharocles megalodon* tooth in good condition may have cost $150; today, prices approach $1,000. Well-preserved mammoth molars could be had for $100; now they are $500 at a minimum. Complete skulls of common oreodonts from the Badlands were obtainable for $50; today a rock-bottom price is $400. Prices for good dinosaur fossil parts, always expensive, have gotten even more so thanks to the popular novels and films *Jurassic Park* and *The Lost World.*

But why buy fossils from someone else, or for that matter, why sell your fossils to others? Collectors resort to the silver pick for many reasons. Most of what is found in the field is in average or below-average condition or appearance. Collectors like to have an excellent specimen or two of local finds. Some avid collectors may want to fill out a collection from their locality, so they buy several specimens that they have not found on their own. Some collectors may find it hard to travel to other places to collect, so they may purchase fossils from other regions. These fossils are called "common" fossils. Some specimens may be one-of-a-kind or exceedingly rare. These are known as "research" fossils.

Generally, fossils are not particularly attractive aesthetically, but some are due to their color, shape, texture, and visual appearance and are viewed as nature's works of art. These unusually attractive specimens are called "decor" fossils. Some fossils appreciate in price more rapidly than others, for any number of reasons. These are known as "investment" fossils.

Individuals and educational institutions are the primary customers for common fossils. Schools have become less important as a market for them because of budget constraints. As a result, a buyer's market has developed for common fossils. This means that prices have not risen much over the years, and they are unlikely to change much, because the supply of common fossils is virtually unlimited and demand is unlikely to change.

Museums and scientific institutions are the largest buyers of research fossils, although they always need a few decor fossils to bring the public in. Budgets are tight for these organizations as well, and competition from private collectors has increased buying pressure, thereby driving up prices and crowding out the budget-constrained museums and institutions. Prices for low-end research fossils are stable to increasing, but high-end research fossil prices are high and headed higher.

The market for decor and investment fossils is extremely strong across the board because of soaring public interest. People who have never, or will never, go out in the field to collect are being drawn in ever-increasing numbers to the combination of natural history and art that decor fossils offer.

According to David Herskowitz, director of natural history with Phillips Auctioneers in New York, "Nearly three-quarters of the buyers of fossils at Phillips' natural history auctions are people who have never collected fossils." By way of example, the following chart (next page) lists the prices paid for representative fossils at a recent Phillips auction.

BUYING AND INVESTING

So now you are ready to test the waters of the fossil business. Just as you need a collecting strategy in the field, you need one indoors too. First and foremost, become knowledgeable about fossils and fossil prices. This can be done by attending rock, mineral, and fossil shows and by visiting

FOSSIL AUCTION PRICES

Description	Sale price ($)
Eagle claw (California — 1 $^1/_2$ inches)	200
Dinosaur footprint (Massachusetts — 5 inches)	375
Coprolite (Washington State — 7 inches)	550
Mastodon molar (Florida — 7 $^1/_2$ x 4 inches)	900
Eurypterus remipes (New York — 20 x 15 inch slab)	1,000
Triceratops vertebra (South Dakota)	1,200
Eremotherium claw (South Carolina — 11 $^1/_2$ inches)	3,500
Ammonite (Alberta — 10 inches, opalescent)	4,000
Dinosaur egg nest (China — 16 eggs)	28,000

Sale prices of fossils from Phillips natural history auction, June 21, 1997.

rock shops, retail stores, museum stores, and auctions. At shows, the best items sell quickly, so be sure to arrive early. Survey what's available and at what prices. Often, identical fossils will be available at different prices because of a dealer's lack of knowledge, inventory problems, profit margins, or cost. Allow plenty of time to do this; it will help you get over the "kid in a candy store" syndrome so that you will be less likely to want to buy one of everything.

Some dealers will be set up in well-lighted, high-traffic areas. Others may be off in a corner or in a tent outside. Don't ignore these away-from-the-mainstream dealers; it costs more to display in good areas, so these dealers may have better prices.

Pay particular attention to dealers who also stock minerals, jewelry, and artifacts. It is hard enough to be knowledgeable about one category, much less three or four. They may not know their merchandise as well as someone who sells only fossils and in some cases may incorrectly identify or price an item to the buyer's benefit. However, the opposite case can occur as well. Additionally, they may have an oversupply in one area and may have priced some merchandise to move.

After doing this several times at different shows, you will have a feel for the pricing of fossils.

Perhaps you just received a bonus or a raise or have saved up some fun money with the intention of buying some fossils. You've learned prices, and you are ready to take the plunge. You arrive early at a show, survey what's available, and decide that you just *have* to buy something. Now what to do? To start with, the best advice is to buy what pleases you. Big, small, pretty, or rare, if you won't enjoy looking at it when you get it home, you are wasting your money.

Other than personal taste, there are several other factors to consider in looking for a fossil that will serve to enhance a collection or will increase in value over time. As indicated before, vertebrate fossils are the fossils of choice if your eye is on investment, but the following guidelines will serve you well with any type of fossil:

1. Buy the best specimen or specimens that you can afford, even if it means leaving with only one or two items.

2. The only time to consider buying something in less-than-excellent condition is if you hear the phrase "Boy, you don't see that very often!" from other potential customers concerning a particular item.

3. Don't get caught up in the "first kid on the block" syndrome. The prices on new kinds of fossils or fossils from new and exotic third-world locations are generally much higher in the first year or two that they are available, when some collectors just have to have one. Over time, the prices decline to more reasonable and sustainable levels. Recent examples include most items from Morocco, Chinese dinosaur eggs, and Dominican amber. These governments control the flow of available fossils and can really pump them out when they are starved for hard currency.

This should help narrow the list of possible purchases. Next, consider the following qualities to help make good decisions. Categories of appreciation potential, in decreasing order, are as follows:

1. *Big and beautiful.* Big and beautiful fossils in excellent condition are always in demand and will appreciate the most.

2. *Small and attractive.* If you are on a more modest budget, small and attractive fossils in excellent condition will do well, too.

3. *Rarity.* Rare fossils are usually not in very good shape or may not appear particularly attractive, but they will always appeal to some group of collectors.

4. *Big and beat up.* Large size always appeals to people, so you may see some appreciation over time, but you are settling for damaged goods. Buyer beware.

5. *Small and beat up.* Only for the kids. Don't bother for your own collection.

Once you purchase a fossil, be sure to get as much information as possible regarding identification, locality, and period or epoch. Lack of full information decreases the value of a specimen.

BUILDING A COLLECTION

Once you start collecting specimens, you will naturally begin to group fossils by organism, location, periods or epochs, and so on. After a while, you will find that some types of fossils are more interesting or attractive to you for various reasons, and you may begin to purchase some fossils that fit your interests. In other words, you begin to build a collection.

A collection built around a particular theme generally has more value than the sum total of its individual parts. For example, an eclectic collection including a large pearly ammonite, an insect in amber, a Badlands skull, a dinosaur footprint, and a leaf imprint may have less value in total than one with a similar number of specimens of different species of ammonites, trilobites, or insects in amber.

The market for a theme collection may be smaller than that for individual specimens, but buyers tend to be more willing to pay up. Another advantage of a theme collection is that all of the specimens need not be in perfect condition. Of course, there is no reason you can't build a theme collection and an eclectic collection as well.

Themes for collections can be as creative as the imagination allows. Typically, a collector will focus on a region, a time period, a family of organisms, or some combination. Other themes include differing characteristics of fossilization or the organism itself. Here are some examples of common themes.

Organisms. Usually something that can be found in quantity and from many different sites, such as shark teeth, ammonites, trilobites, fish, or petrified wood.

Body parts. Skulls, jaws, teeth, bones, or claws.

Locality. Usually many species from one well-known site or formation, such as the Green River, Mazon Creek, or the Big Badlands.

Time period. It doesn't matter which period or epoch, although Devonian, Cretaceous, and Pleistocene seem to be the most popular, and Ordovician, Silurian, and Paleocene seem to be the least popular.

Geologic properties. What would be common fossils become decor fossils when they are pyritized, opalized, or fluorescent.

Pathology. Most collectors toss malformed fossils away, but to some they are highly treasured. Skulls, teeth, and bones that show pathology are most popular.

TRADING, DONATING, OR SELLING YOUR FOSSILS

The day may come when, for any number of reasons, you wish to dispose of some or all of your fossils. You have a number of options, including trading, donating, or selling your fossils. What ultimately determines the price you get will be how desperate you are to sell them. Being knowledgeable about fossil prices will ensure that you receive full value.

Trading

If the only reason you wish to dispose of your fossils is that you are tired of them, consider trading with other collectors. Many fossil and mineral clubs have swap meets for just such reasons. When trading by mail, it is wise to suggest a small initial trade. If you are satisfied with what you receive, you will feel more comfortable with a larger trade afterward.

Donating

If you wish to leave a legacy in some small way, donating fossils to a museum or school is a good option. The general perception may be that your fossils will be packed in a box in the back room of the museum and forgotten, but the truth is that the back rooms of museums are where scientists and researchers do the truly important work. Though your donation may not be displayed, it will be studied and cataloged and better cared for than you can do on your own. As an alternative, try contacting local science teachers. If you find one who is enthusiastic about fossils and will utilize them, you have found a good new home for your surplus items. In either case, you may be entitled to a tax deduction for the full market value of the fossils.

Selling for Cash

Dealers

Fossil dealers are a good source to investigate if you wish to sell quickly. Local and regional dealers can be found through fossil clubs. Larger dealers can be found at fossil shows or through advertisements in general science or earth science magazines. They usually have ready cash and will tell you quickly if they are interested. To a dealer, fossils are a business first and a hobby second. A dealer will buy fossils only if they can be resold at a higher price. This is no different than any other merchandising business. Thus, you likely will be offered wholesale prices, which may be significantly lower than the retail.

Individuals

If you want full value, or nearly so, for your fossils, there are a number of options. Check with fossil club members as to whether anyone is interested in buying what you have, but be discreet; avoid appearing desperate. If you have a large number of items, consider renting a table at a local fossil or mineral show. Rental fees can be as low as $50 for a table. Some collectors have even done well at flea markets. Classified ads in *Lapidary Journal, Earth,* and fossil club newsletters can also be effective.

Auctions

For those collectors with valuable or unusual specimens, natural history auctions are an increasingly popular option. The largest auction in the United States is conducted twice a year in New York by Phillips. Asking prices have ranged from $150 to $1 million. There are charges and fees, and your specimens will be out of your physical possession for a period of time, but this is probably the best single way to reach motivated individual and institutional buyers. If you are in the New York area during an auction, visit if only to see the marvelous display of fossils. Who knows, you might see something you want to purchase.

For most people interested in fossils, buying, selling, or trading a fossil is a one-time event. It's either in your collection or out of it, and little thought is given to where it came from or where it went. But serious collectors know that sometimes a fossil may have more mileage on it than you put on your car in a year. Consider the following true story.

A certain elephant mandible with beautiful agatized green teeth was found in a Florida phosphate mine by a first-time collector in 1976. He immediately sold the jaw with two teeth to his guide, and friend, for $200. The guide was also a fossil dealer, and he sold the jaw to another dealer in Orlando for $500. One month later, the second dealer traded the jaw to a collector in Lakeland, Florida, for $700 worth of fossils.

The collector held the piece for almost six months, when he decided to trade it back to the Orlando dealer for a small collection of elephant teeth, and the original piece went up another $300, making the jaw worth $1,000. The Orlando dealer then sold the jaw to a collector in Brandon, Florida, for $1,500, who sold it back to the first collector in Lakeland for $1,700, who then sold it back to the original guide and dealer for $2,000, who then sold it back to the Orlando dealer, who sold it to a Riverview, Florida, collector for $2,400.

The jaw stayed with the Riverview collector for nearly a year, until it went on the road again back to the Orlando dealer for $3,000. The Orlando dealer took the jaw to the Tucson Gem and Mineral Show and sold it to a collector from Japan for $3,500.

About three years elapsed from the time the elephant jaw was found to the time it was sold in Tucson. Needless to say, with all that mileage, its warranty expired after the fourth owner!

—F. G.

10

Great Amateurs and Great Finds

We will never know who the first person was to pick up a fossil and wonder about its origins. Since fossils have been found along with the remains of Stone Age people, they must have been the first fossil collectors.

The science of paleontology and the study of fossils are not much more than two hundred years old. Many people have been drawn to fossils, both as their life's work and as a passionate hobby.

Most fossil-collecting books focus on the works of the great academic and professional paleontologists. More than other branches of science, however, paleontology owes a debt of gratitude to amateur enthusiasts, whose tireless efforts and selflessness have taken this science to levels unachievable by university and museum professionals alone.

Some of the greatest amateur finds were the result of many hours in the field and in libraries. Some were made by people who had no previous interest in fossils and happened to stumble onto something fantastic. Some of these finds were made by one-time wonders; others were made by frequent finders.

This chapter is dedicated to the great amateurs, the yet-to-become great amateurs, and those who may never achieve fame but who still contribute to the science.

THOMAS JEFFERSON

Perhaps the most famous amateur fossil collector of all time achieved his fame not as a collector, but as the author of the Declaration of Independence and as the third president of the United States. Thomas Jefferson's greatness as a statesman and in his many avocations is well known. However, few people realize his interest in and passion for fossils. In a letter to Meriwether Lewis, he once intimated that fossils were possibly the most fascinating pieces of natural history.

Jefferson had little opportunity to collect personally, primarily obtaining fossils collected by others. In 1797, while vice president of the United States and president of the American Philosophical Society, Jefferson presented one of the first papers on vertebrate paleontology in America, entitled "A Memoir on the Discovery of Certain Bones of a Quadruped of the Clawed Kind in the Western Parts of Virginia."

Jefferson had been given three large fossilized claws of an unknown animal that had been found in a cave. He studied them and decided that they belonged to a giant type of carnivore, which he named *Megalonyx,* or "great claw." It was later determined that these were the claws of a large, extinct, herbivorous ground sloth. Despite the misidentification, the name *Megalonyx jeffersoni* is still used for the Pleistocene ground sloth that once roamed much of North America.

As president, Jefferson sent Lewis and Clark west on their famous expedition to find a route to the Pacific Ocean. Jefferson believed that living creatures of the type whose fossils he had collected might be found out west, so he also instructed Lewis and Clark to search for them. Several years after completion of the expedition, Jefferson sent Clark to Big Bone Lick in Kentucky to recover fossils that were known to be plentiful there. Clark shipped back more than three hundred bones, most of them coming from mastodons. Also during his presidency, Jefferson turned the east wing of the White House into one of the first paleontological museums and laboratories in the country.

MARY ANNING

Mary Anning's father was a carpenter in the town of Lyme Regis, on the southern coast of England. To supplement his income, he would collect fossils, primarily Jurassic ammonites, from the nearby ocean cliffs and beaches and sell them to curious vacationers as well as natural history buffs. When her father died after her tenth birthday, Mary continued to collect fossils and sell them to help support her family. Ultimately, she became one of the most famous collectors of all time.

Some of the incomparable finds attributed to Mary Anning include the world's first complete ichthyosaur, which she found and excavated in 1810 at the age of twelve; the first complete plesiosaur, in 1823; and the first complete British pterosaur, in 1828.

GIDEON AND MARY MANTELL

Mary Mantell was the wife of Gideon Mantell, a physician and lifelong fossil enthusiast. He was recognized as one of the great amateur collectors of his time. His fame, however, is due in large part to a discovery by his wife in 1822. She had been out for a walk along a country road near their home in Sussex, England, when she spotted two large fossil teeth. She showed them to her husband, who studied them. More bones were later found nearby. He noticed similarities to the teeth and bones of the living iguana, and in 1825 he named this giant "lizard" *Iguanodon*. It was later recognized as the second dinosaur ever found.

FRANCIS TULLY

Francis Tully was an avid fisherman who frequented the small lakes around the coal-mining region near his home in Lockport, Illinois, in the early 1960s. When the fishing was slow, he would break open the rusty brown rocks, called concretions, that were scattered among the spoil piles in the strip mines.

From time to time, he would find fossilized plant material and marine organisms. On one bad fishing day, he cracked open one of these rocks to find something that he had not seen before. He took the specimen to experts at the Field Museum of Natural History in Chicago. They were not sure what it was either, but they did realize that it was like nothing they had ever seen.

Not only did this fossil receive a new species name, but it also resulted in a new genus, family, order, and phylum. The "Tully monster," *Tullimonstrum gregarium*, turned out to be an incredible catch on a day when the fish weren't biting.

ARTHUR LOY AND JAN CUMMINGS

One day in 1979, Arthur Loy and Jan Cummings were out hiking, bound for an Indian petroglyph site in the Ojito Wilderness Study Area west of Albuquerque, New Mexico. Just short of their destination, Loy spotted some huge bones partially exposed on a sandstone ledge. They could only be dinosaur bones, but none had ever been found in that part of the state.

They reported the find shortly thereafter. Not until six years later, when a formal excavation began, did they learn that they had discovered the longest dinosaur ever found to that point, *Seismosaurus.*

BECKY AND FRANK HYNE
Under the heading "Great Donors" in the Smithsonian Institution's 150th Anniversary Yearbook, published in 1996, is a color photograph of a woman and a man wearing hardhats. By some oversight, their names were left out of the text, but fossil collectors from all over the country know who they are. To many, the woman is "the lady that drives the bus" and the man is "her husband." At the Smithsonian Institution, they are regarded as two of the greatest donors of all time. Becky and Frank Hyne have given more than twenty thousand scientifically significant fossil specimens to the Smithsonian since 1974, when they first started collecting fossils, and they continue to add to that total regularly. "We know what they are studying, and we send them anything we know they'll be interested in," explains Becky.

Becky and Frank are most unusual in that they are a wife and husband who both enjoy fossil collecting. According to Frank, "Becky is the better fossil hunter and by far the better classifier. She knows what everything is. And she's my hero, too!" However, though they both enjoy fossil collecting, they don't particularly enjoy doing it side by side. "We just aggravate each other, so we go our separate ways when we go out in the field," says Frank.

In fact, Becky does drive a bus. It happens to be the bus that all fossil collectors must take into the Lee Creek phosphate mine near Aurora, North Carolina. More than six hundred species of mostly Miocene and Pliocene fossils have been found in the mine, making it one of the most famous collecting sites in the world. And though the mine's ownership has changed hands over the years, corporate generosity still provides collectors belonging to recognized fossil clubs access to collect and keep anything that they find.

Becky and Frank, who is retired, are responsible for safely transporting all collectors into and out of the mine and ensuring that everyone adheres to the strict safety rules of this working facility. The fact that amateur collectors are allowed in at all in this day and age is testament to Becky and Frank's efforts, even at the risk of alienating some collectors who feel that the mine's rules do not pertain to them.

Becky not only is responsible for the transportation and safety of collectors, but also feels responsible for educating and helping them as well.

"If someone comes up to me and shows me something that's not a very good specimen, I tell them that they can do better and suggest where they should look."

True to form, Becky and Frank were quite a distance apart while collecting in the mine when Becky's "find of a lifetime" occurred. The Lee Creek Mine is perhaps best known for the relative abundance of huge teeth of the giant white shark, *Carcharocles megalodon*. Becky saw a broken one, bent over to pick it up, and turned over a large shell nearby, only to find another tooth—this one perfect—and then a third one. Frank was some distance away, and she had to yell six times before she got his attention. As he climbed up, down, and around the huge spoil piles that separated them, he thought to himself, "Boy, this better be good."

Indeed it was. By the end of the day, they had found eight giant teeth. It took four more days, with a lot of help from friends, to completely work the area, resulting in a total of forty teeth (twenty-five in pristine condition), as well as seal, whale, dolphin, and turtle material. Given the close proximity of the teeth and their nearly identical size, it is assumed that all came from the same animal—the finest assemblage of *C. megalodon* teeth from one adult animal in the world.

More than anything, it's the thrill of the hunt that excites Becky and Frank. They love the outdoors and travel all over the country to collect. "We've met lots of people and have had visitors from England, France, Sweden, Norway, and India. Some even stay with us. We just got hooked on fossiling, and it's wonderful that we share this together."

What does it take to be a great fossil hunter? Says Becky, "Perseverance, a love of the outdoors, and be sure to investigate every bone and tooth you find." Says Frank with a smile, "Good shoes."

GEORGE W. POWELL, JR.

On July 10, 1996, a special ceremony marking the formal donation of an unusual set of fossils was held at the National Museum of Natural History at the Smithsonian Institution in Washington, D.C. At that ceremony, George W. Powell, Jr., was described by the assistant director of the museum, Dr. David L. Pawson, as having donated the "fossil shark equivalent of the Mona Lisa." George wore his letter carrier's uniform to the ceremony that day because he "had a very special delivery to make."

After having caught their limit on a fishing trip along the Potomac River in 1980, George and a friend explored the riverbanks and began finding fossils. Not only did he hook his limit, but he was hooked on fossils from that day on. Over the following years, he read about, hunted for, and asked experts about fossils in all of his spare time. He developed a reputation as one of the best fossil hunters in the mid-Atlantic coastal plain, and his favorite site was the Lee Creek Mine near Aurora, North Carolina.

In the summer of 1992, two extremely rare shark teeth of the extinct false mako shark, *Parotodus benedeni,* were found in the Lee Creek Mine and were brought to his attention. He obtained permission to return to the mine to search for more. On the first and second days, he found 63 more teeth. During the next eighteen months, with help from Dr. Bretton Kent of the University of Maryland and some volunteers, 49 more teeth were recovered. Given the proximity and similarity of size, all 114 teeth are assumed to have come from a single adult *Parotodus benedeni*—the only find like it in the world.

He spurned offers of large sums of money and decided to donate the entire find to the Smithsonian Institution. "It was a hard decision but it was a quick one, and the right one. Someone actually called me on the phone and told me I was a horse's ass for donating it instead of selling it. But I did it because if I didn't, who would? This way, two hundred years from now, someone can study these fossils and determine the answers to questions we didn't even think of."

George feels strongly that individuals should be able to collect and own fossils. Although he rarely buys fossils, preferring to trade with other collectors for them, he sees nothing wrong with that either. But when it comes to something scientifically important, he believes it's the responsibility of amateur collectors to "do the right thing."

Sharing his finds and experiences with others, especially children, is very important to him. "If I can get a kid to spend five minutes looking at my stuff, that's five minutes less outside where the real trouble is."

About fossil collecting, he says: "I have been lucky, and luck does play a big part of it. Knowledge is important, too. The more you know, the more luck you make for yourself. Anyone can do what I have done, but what has made me better at it than most is that I use all the tools [knowledge and information] available to me. I've studied the textures and compositions of different sediments; I know what I'm looking for; I plan where I am going; I take into account subtle differences in color and whether it's a sunny or overcast day; I've learned which plants grow in sediment that is likely to yield good finds; I've learned which plants send their roots down and which send them sideways; I've even studied how dragline buckets empty their contents." And there is plenty more.

Lightning struck again for George Powell three years after the start of his "*Parotodus* adventure," when he and two other experienced collectors walked past a small, white object protruding out of the sediment at Lee

Creek. It looked unusual to him, so he stopped to investigate while the others, certain that it was a common find, continued on. The tusk and skull of what turned out to be a new species of walrus now reside in the Smithsonian as well.

BEN WALLER

There aren't many amateur fossil collectors who become the stuff of legend in paleontology, much less in other endeavors, but Ben Waller, of Ocala, Florida, was one such man.

Ben Waller flew Navy jet fighters and was an accomplished race car driver, judo instructor, herpetologist, Hollywood stuntman, and underwater diver. He served as chief of operations of civil defense in Ocala, which included the physically and emotionally difficult task of retrieving the bodies of divers who drowned while exploring the many underwater caves that surround the area. But it was his love of diving that brought him his fame.

Florida's Silver Springs tourist attraction, in Ocala, is the world's largest formation of clear artesian springs, and its glass-bottom boat tours draw hundreds of thousands of visitors annually. Over the years, the attraction has also drawn many Hollywood producers and directors to film at the site. Ben's diving reputation made him the person of choice as film advisor and stuntman, and he worked with Elvis Presley, Rock Hudson, Richard Harris, Lee Majors, and other television and film stars of the day. For many years he was the dive coach of Lloyd Bridges on the popular 1960s television show "Sea Hunt." The one regret in his film career was turning down the role of the monster in *The Creature from the Black Lagoon*, which became one of the most successful science fiction movies of all time.

However, his Hollywood exploits pale in comparison to his dual contributions to the sciences of archaeology and paleontology. An entire book could be devoted to a biography of his years of effort and discovery in Florida's waters, as well as his teaching and motivation of countless others who followed in his wake.

Both fossils and Indian artifacts can be found in Florida's rivers and underwater caves. It is unusual for a serious Indian artifact collector to find more than several paleo-Indian (9,000 years of age and older) projectile points in a lifetime. Ben found more of them than any other individual known, professional or amateur. A previously unknown type of Indian artifact, the Waller knife, was named in his honor.

For a fossil collector, finding a new animal species is the ultimate achievement, one that few collectors ever experience. Ben Waller was responsible for more than ten new species of extinct animals, one of which, a nearly 10-foot-tall, flightless, predatory bird, was named *Titanis walleri* in his honor.

But it was also his careful and scientific approach to the excavation of the Indian and fossil sites he found that contributed to his unofficial title, "The Father of Underwater Archaeology and Paleontology." Yet even with all of his fame, he remained one of the kindest, warmest, most patient, and honorable of men.

Ben Waller died in 1994 surrounded by his family. Today, the mention of his name among people who knew him brings both sadness and joy to their faces; sadness, because he is no longer here, and joy, because of the opportunity they had to know such a great man.

BOB DENTON

Bob Denton discovered dinosaurs when he was a toddler living in New Jersey. "The family story is that when I was still in a high chair, the only way they could get me to eat was to distract me by showing me pictures of dinosaurs in the World Book encyclopedia." More than two decades later, he discovered real dinosaurs—and much more.

During the summer between his freshman and sophomore years in college, Bob worked as a field assistant on a paleontological expedition conducted by Harvard University's Museum of Comparative Zoology. He spent that summer in the Bighorn Basin of Wyoming, hunting for early Cretaceous mammals and learning the scientific approach to paleontology under the leadership of Chuck Schaff, his first mentor.

After Bob left college, he moved around several times, then went to work as a research scientist at Johnson and Johnson back in New Jersey in 1978. "Almost right away, I said I'd like to go out and try my hand at finding some fossils." He started frequenting the well-known sites in New Jersey and found only the common fossils. During this time, he met and developed a relationship with Dave Parris of the New Jersey State Museum, whom he considers his second mentor.

Early in the summer of 1980, Bob and a former roommate, Bob O'Neill, went hunting for fossils in an unnamed tributary of Crosswicks Creek near Ellisdale, New Jersey. The late Cretaceous Marshalltown Formation was known to be exposed there, but no fossils had ever been reported.

They found nothing as well, but Bob Denton says he "had this feeling in my gut that there was something here." Not only that, but he remembered what Chuck Schaff had said back in Wyoming. "If you go where other people have found lots of stuff, and you find something, odds are you're going to find what they found. You might find something different, but you're not going to get your place in the sun that way. On the other hand, if you look in formations where nobody's ever found anything, and you do find something, then you're on the map."

In early fall, Bob convinced Bob O'Neill to visit the creek once again. "Not more than twenty or thirty feet up the little tributary from the main creek, I looked down and my eyes went wide because there, lying right in the middle of the streambed, was a chunk of fossil turtle bone, easily the size of my hand. I walked about twenty more feet, and there was a piece of dinosaur bone maybe five or six inches long. It was a portion of a neck vertebra of a hadrosaur. I walked another ten feet and there was another piece of bone."

They took the three bones to Dave Parris, who suggested that they continue to search the site regularly. For the next three years, after every heavy rain, they would walk the stream and find more pieces of bone. The collection now numbered almost seventy specimens.

In March 1984, 11 inches of rain fell in a twenty-four-hour period; Bob refers to this as "the Great Event." The stream became a massive torrent that cut into the elusive productive layer. As soon as the water level dropped, they returned. "There was bone everywhere. Within two weeks, the collection went from almost seventy specimens to over five hundred."

At that point, Bob Denton and Dave Parris decided that this was something truly special and should be formally studied. A grant from the National Geographic Society was awarded. To date, there are now about twenty-five thousand specimens from the site. Nearly all of the specimens have been collected by the two Bobs alone, and all have been donated to the State Museum of New Jersey.

Not only are individual dinosaur fossils abundant, but the site has turned out to be one of the best Cretaceous terrestrial microfaunal assemblages in the world. The most exciting aspect of the site is that nearly all of the smaller fossils that can be compared to other specimens are new species.

Bob explains further: "During the late Cretaceous, North America was split by an inland sea. Prior to Ellisdale, the prevailing view was that once a terrestrial site was found in the eastern continent and produced fossils that were comparable to known sites from the western continent, the fauna would show great similarity. The Ellisdale site is currently the only known site found in the East. Though some of the dinosaurs are the same as those in the West, the microfauna [reptiles, amphibians, and mammals] are very different. It's as if we discovered a lost continent."

Since the site is in New Jersey, they jokingly refer to eastern North America of the Late Cretaceous as "the Lost Continent of Greater New Jersey."

Bob's work took him away from New Jersey in 1995. Leaving the area, plus the necessity of studying and describing all that has been found, means that he now has little time for collecting at the Ellisdale site. His work takes him to Arizona for periods of time now. True to form, in 1996, while Bob was hunting for fossils in a Cretaceous formation of New Mexico that "was considered essentially barren, we hit into a booming dinosaur fauna." And history repeats itself.

Bob's advice for those just starting out:

• Find a trained professional paleontologist to be a mentor. There is so much to do and so few people that most professionals are happy to take a beginner under their wing.

• Read as much as you can about paleontology, especially the scientific literature.

• Hunt in formations where no one has found anything. It's worked for him—twice.

WAYNE A. COVINGTON

Since 1970, Wayne A. Covington has lived at the same address: It is likely that he will live there for the rest of his life. Wayne is an inmate at the State Correctional Institute at Graterford, Pennsylvania; a most unusual place to find a fossil collector, but Wayne, nicknamed Fang, is a most unusual person.

Between 1970 and 1980, Wayne lived inside the prison compound. During that time, he worked with the prison psychologist and helped administer and interpret intelligence and personality tests. Wayne also earned a bachelor's degree in sociology from Villanova University through its degree program offered to staff, guards, and inmates at Graterford. During this time, he met and developed a close relationship with Dr. James McKenna at Villanova, which continues to the present.

In 1980, Wayne was given the opportunity to live in the Outside Service Unit (OSU) outside of the compound. At first he worked at grounds maintenance, then at the prison dairy. One day, while walking in a cow pen, he looked down and saw a round object outlined in the dirt. He picked it up, rubbed off the dirt, and realized he'd found an old coin. It turned out to be a 1721 King George I halfpence in perfect condition. Wayne then became attuned to the round mental image and began finding many coins, most coming from the early 1800s.

Part of Wayne's job included the responsibility to retrieve cows that had escaped from the dairy pens and to post no hunting and trespassing signs all over the 1,700 acres of prison grounds. In crossing the plowed fields of the prison farm, Wayne not only found coins, but also isolated Indian artifacts.

As he found more artifacts, he started taking an interest in archaeology. With further study, he became adept at recognizing patterns of artifacts that indicated actual campsites. In fact, Wayne has now registered twelve historic sites on the prison grounds. "Most of them are archaic and woodland sites, but I did find one paleo-Indian point. It's the easternmost discovery of this type of point in the country."

On November 2, 1993, Wayne was walking the grounds to replace posted signs when he walked down a gully and realized he was walking on a gray shalelike material. "I remember thinking to myself that this looked like argillite [the material that many arrowheads and points are made of], so I gave it a whack with my hammer to see if it was. The rock planed perfectly, and there was the positive and the negative of a dinosaur footprint."

He reported the find to the prison administration and received permission to investigate further. A team from the State Museum of Pennsylvania arrived several weeks later to excavate the footprint and a second trackway Wayne had found in a nearby gully. The State Museum did not have the staff to undertake a dig, so it was left to Wayne and other inmates in the OSU to work the site. "The superintendent [Donald T. Vaughn] was very supportive of the project, and things really began to take off when Ted Daeschler [collections manager for vertebrate paleontology, Academy of Natural Sciences in Philadelphia] became the site supervisor. He was able to supply the tools, information, and advice that we really needed." But as time passed, the inmates that were helping had to leave the OSU. "Ahmed Sabur, especially, was a big help early on, but since 1995, I've been doing it by myself. I'm usually able to put in a couple of hours a day, four or five times a week after I finish my job in the dairy."

Since the first discovery, a total of fourteen trackway sites have been found on the prison grounds. "I gave up counting after a while, but I'd estimate we've found close to 1,500 actual tracks." Paul Olsen, of Columbia University, one of the foremost authorities on dinosaur tracks in the world, has studied the prints and the site and has determined that they date to the late Triassic (Passaic Formation) about 220 million years ago. Three categories of tracks have been identified: *Atreipus*, ornithopod-type, herbivorous dinosaurs; *Grallator*, carnivorous dinosaurs believed to be *Coelophysis* or something similar; and *Rhynchosauroides*, little, scurrying lizards. Additional tracks have been found, but their identification is still unclear.

The best finds have been sent to museums, and good finds have gone to universities and schools that request them. "I'd gone as far as I could with college some time ago, so this has been a new learning experience for me," says Wayne. "I've got a stack of letters from elementary school kids thanking me and asking questions, and that's what's really gratifying. Most of the things I've found, I've tried to put in a historical or biblical time frame; old coins from the time of the Revolutionary War, Indian artifacts from the time of Jesus, Abraham, or the ancient Greeks, but 220 million years ago is just unimaginable. I can't put that into a point of reference."

According to Ted Daeschler, "This site is similar to others in the area," but when asked what makes it special, he cites three factors:

• The preservation of the major trackways at Graterford is better than at most of the other sites.

• Although both dinosaur species were bipedal (walked on two legs), many handprints have been found at Graterford.

• The site has been worked essentially by one man who has exhibited qualities that are rare under normal circumstances, much less in prison: a thirst for knowledge and understanding and the sheer force of will to continue the backbreaking work necessary to more fully understand the Graterford site.

Wayne has received a great deal of notoriety as a result of his work. He has been the subject of numerous newspaper and television features, and CNN ran the story on Christmas day of 1994.

"Since I'm a lifer, the only way that I can leave here is if the governor commutes my sentence." If that ever happens, "I've received a scholarship from Villanova University for graduate study, and I have a standing offer as a lecturer in Drexel University's Criminal Justice Program. I'd really like to be a teacher," he says. Wayne may not realize it, but he is one already.

PART TWO

Fossil Identification

Vertebrate Fossils

Fossils shown are at actual size unless otherwise noted after corresponding captions.

Section 1A • *Jaws and Teeth*

Most animal skulls contain two jaws. The maxilla, or upper jaw, is fused to the skull below the nasal cavity, and it is immobile. The mandible, or lower jaw, is movable and is attached to the skull via hinge joints just in front of the ears. In common usage, the term *jaw* usually refers to the lower jaw. Dentition refers to the kinds of teeth and their arrangement in the jaws.

While the shapes and sizes of teeth differ enormously, enamel is the primary indicator of a fossil tooth. Enamel is the hard and smooth outside layer of a tooth. Inside the enamel is a bonelike layer of dentine, which also forms the root. The innermost portion of a tooth contains soft pulp and nerves, which rarely fossilize.

Incisors are the teeth at the front of the jaw in mammals. They are usually sharp-edged and used for cutting or nipping. Carnivores, omnivores, and perissodactyls (horses, for example) have incisors in the maxilla and mandible. Artiodactyls (bison, for example) have them only in the mandible.

Canines are usually conical and pointed, and they are located between the incisors and the first premolars. They are designed for gripping and puncturing. Few herbivores have canines; instead, there is usually a gap (diastema) between the incisors and premolars.

Premolars are usually flattish in herbivores and are designed for grinding. Carnivore premolars are designed for either cutting or crushing.

95

Molars are the last teeth in the jaw. Herbivore molars are usually flat grinding teeth. Their upper molars are generally square; the lower molars are generally rectangular. In carnivores, the first lower molar and the fourth upper premolar are called carnassial teeth. They are knife-edged for cutting or shearing. The last molar in some carnivores may be more blunt and serve to crack bones. Omnivore molars are somewhat intermediate, as might be expected.

Carnivore mandibles usually exhibit some curvature. This allows greater pressure to be exerted at the front of the jaw, where the canines are used for holding or puncturing. Herbivore mandibles are usually long and flat and increase in size from the front of the jaw to the back. This allows more pressure to be exerted from the middle to the back of the jaw, where the grinding teeth are.

JAWS: MANDIBLES AND MOUTHPLATES

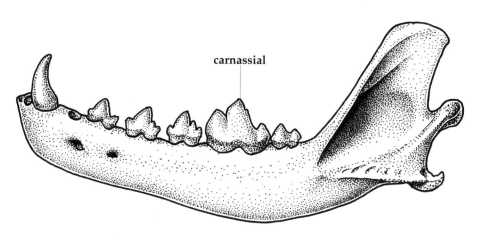

Canis **sp., wolf. Incisors (not shown) and canines used for grasping and puncturing, premolars and molars (carnassials) used for cutting and shearing.** *(x ^{2}/$_3$)*

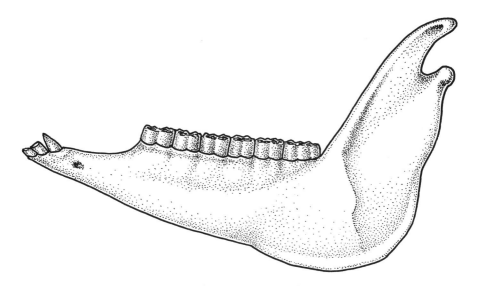

Equus sp., horse. Incisors used for grazing, diastema (no canines), premolars and molars used for grinding. *(x ¹/₄)*

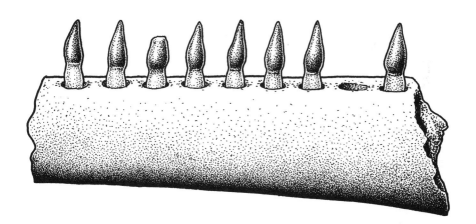

Dolphin/porpoise (species unknown). Identical teeth and unchanging jawbone, grasping (they swallow prey whole). *(x ²/₃)*

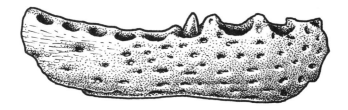

Alligator mississippiensis, American alligator. Teeth of similar shape throughout the mouth, although size varies; shape of jaw changes along its length. Pitting on the bone is the true indicator. Grasping. Partial jaw.

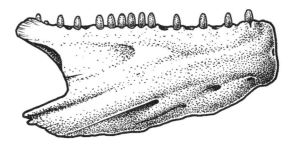

Pomatus sp., bluefish. Gasping and puncture. Typical bony fish jaw.

Myliobatis sp., eagle ray. Pavement teeth have remained articulated. Crushing. Mouthplate.

Diodon sp., porcupinefish. This fish has no teeth. Crushing. Upper mouthplate. *(x ¹/₂)*

Phyllodus sp., wrasse. Crushing. Mouthplate.

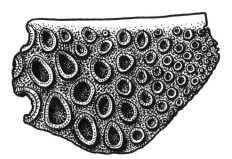

Pogonias sp., drumfish. The "teeth" rarely stay attached to the plate. The true teeth are farther back in the mouth. Crushing. Mouthplate.

TEETH

Cartilaginous Fish

Sharks, skates, rays, sawfish, and their kin are all fish that lost the ability to produce bone. Instead, their bodies are supported by tough cartilage. Sharks developed torpedolike shapes and teeth with enamel to eat flesh. Skates and rays developed a flattened profile with bony mouthplates to crush shells and bottom-dwelling arthropods. Sawfish also developed a flattened profile but grew long snouts with teeth on the outer edges, which are used to impale or stun prey.

Sharks

Primitive sharks first appeared about 400 million years ago. It was during the Jurassic, however, that the first modern sharks appeared. It is estimated that the modern mature shark produces about twenty thousand teeth in its lifetime, so it is no surprise that shark teeth are by far the most numerous vertebrate fossils to be found.

Shark teeth have a root, consisting of a dentinelike material, and a crown, consisting of enamel or enameloid material on the outside and dentine filling the inside. The view of each tooth shown here is commonly thought to be the front of the tooth, but in fact, it is the back, or lingual, side—the side that faces the throat when it reaches its final position in the jaw.

Shark tooth identification can be frustrating. Though the teeth of some species are uniform throughout the mouth, many species have significant differences between upper and lower, front and back, and juvenile and adult teeth. Additionally, there may be differences among individuals of the same species, and teeth of some species may be indistinguishable from one another except by an expert. Throw in worn or broken teeth, and you may just give up.

Nevertheless, shark tooth collecting is both fun and exciting (remember, these teeth belonged to killers), and though you may not be able to identify the species of a tooth, in most cases it is possible to generalize as to the common name of a specimen.

Shark teeth are grouped here by adult tooth size. The first group includes species whose teeth frequently exceed 2 inches in slant height. All fishermen, including fossil shark fishermen, tend to "adjust" the length of their catch. As such, large shark teeth are measured by their slant height as opposed to the vertical height. The slant height measures the length from the tip of the enamel to the tip of the root along the side of the tooth, rather than the vertical height from top to bottom.

SHARK TEETH, GROUPED BY SIZE
A. Broad, triangular teeth, commonly exceeding 2 inches in slant height

Otodus obliquus, giant mackerel shark. Paleocene to Eocene. Up to 4 inches. Note the presence of side cusps, bourlette (wide groove between root and enameloid), U-shaped notch in root, no serrations. *(x ⁴/5)*

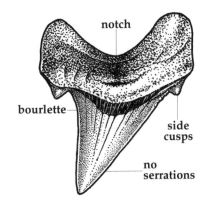

Carcharocles auriculatus, Eocene. Up to 4 inches. *C. auriculatus* is believed to have evolved from *Otodus;* exhibits all of the same characteristics of *Otodus,* plus the addition of fine serrations. *(x ³·⁵/5)*

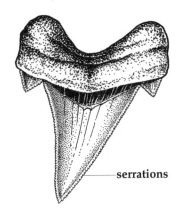

Carcharocles megalodon, giant white shark. Miocene to Pliocene. Over 7 inches. Body may have exceeded 60 feet. Believed to have evolved from *C. auriculatus;* exhibits the same characteristics except for the lack of side cusps. *(x ⁴/5)*

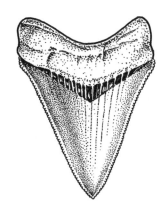

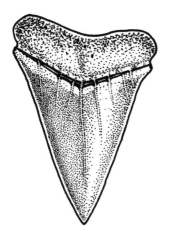

Isurus hastalis, **mako. Oligocene to Pliocene. Up to 3¹/₂ inches, lacks serrations, bourlette, and U-shaped notch in root.**

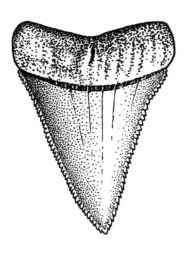

Carcharodon carcharias, **the living great white shark. Miocene to present. Up to 3 inches. Believed to have evolved from** *I. hastalis;* **teeth indistinguishable except for the presence of coarse serrations.**

B. Smaller, broad or daggerlike teeth

Squalicorax kaupi, **crow shark. Cretaceous; very common during late Cretaceous.**

Striatolamia macrota, sand tiger. Paleocene to Eocene. This tooth form causes more confusion than any other. It is very similar to *Scapanorhynchus,* the goblin shark of the Cretaceous, and other sand tigers of various epochs. Three genera, containing more than fifteen species of fossil sand tigers, are known from North America, including the living species, *Carcharias taurus.* Given that finds may be partially worn, stratigraphic location may be more helpful than visual inspection in identifying the genus and species.

Hemipristis serra, snaggletooth shark. Oligocene to Pliocene. Characterized by heavy serrations.

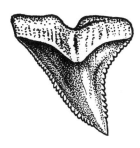

Notorhynchus primigenius, seven-gilled cow shark. Oligocene to Pliocene. Generally less than 1 inch in length, and mesial edge has small cusps.

mesial edge

mesial edge

Hexanchus gigas, six-gilled cow shark. Miocene to Pliocene. Cow sharks are primitive sharks exhibiting seven or six gill slits rather than the five slits of advanced sharks. Their teeth are distinctive in that they are roughly rectangular, with multiple cusps. *H. gigas* may be confused with *Notorhynchus,* although *H. gigas* is generally larger than 1 inch in length, and the mesial edges of its teeth have fine serrations.

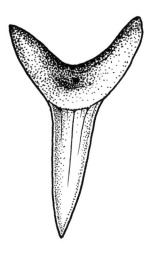

Isurus desori, mako. Miocene to Pliocene. Juvenile teeth typically have side cusps that resemble sand tiger teeth.

Galeocerdo contortus, tiger. Oligocene to Miocene. Appears pathological, as enameloid portion is
twisted.

Galeocerdo cuvier, tiger. Pliocene to Recent. The living species of tiger shark.

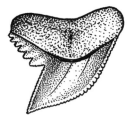

Negaprion eurybathrodon, lem-
on. Miocene. Easily confused
with lower teeth of *Carcharhinus egertoni.* It takes an expert
and a magnifying glass to tell
the difference.

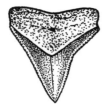

Carcharhinus egertoni, gray. Miocene. Gray sharks are the most successful of all living species, with more than twenty-five species described. Very abundant as fossils. Most fossil species are from the Miocene, but the genus stretches from Eocene to the present. Species identification is very difficult, given the small size of the teeth and the similarity among species.

Sawfish

Sawfish have flattened, sharklike bodies with elongated snouts, or rostra. Rostral teeth growing along the side of the snout are used to stun or impale its prey.

Ischyrhiza mira. Cretaceous. Conical.

Pristis sp., Eocene to recent. Lateral and posterior views.

Rays

Aetobatis sp., duck-billed ray. Miocene to Pleistocene. V-shaped pavement "teeth." *(x ¹/₂)*

Myliobatis sp., eagle ray. Cretaceous to Pleistocene. Straight individual pavement "teeth." *(x ¹/₂)*

Fish

Sphyraena sp., barracuda. Cretaceous to recent. Very thin teeth. *(x 2)*

Reptiles

Crocodiles and birds are the only surviving descendants of the archosaurs (ruling reptiles). The first crocodiles appeared in the Triassic. The first alligators and caimans appeared in the Paleocene.

Thecachampsa **sp., crocodile. Paleocene to Miocene.**

Plesiosaur (species unknown), marine reptile, Jurassic to Cretaceous. Long-necked plesiosaurs probably inhabited the surfaces of the oceans; short-necked plesiosaurs (also called pliosaurs) probably hunted in deeper water. Both types may have reached 50 feet in length. Swam with flippers as marine turtles do. Crowns are curved and striated. *(x ¹/₂)*

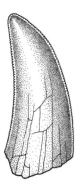

Allosaurid-type (species unknown), carnivorous dinosaur. Jurassic to Cretaceous. Teeth are curved and serrated, perfectly designed for slicing. *(x ¹/₂)*

Mosasaur (species unknown), marine lizard. Cretaceous. Appeared abruptly and was widespread, becoming extinct at the end of the Cretaceous. Some species preyed on ammonites (ammonite fossils have been found with tooth marks that match mosasaur jaws); other species preyed on marine vertebrates. Reached lengths of 40 feet. Crowns are curved, robust, not striated. *(x ³/₅)*

Cetiosaurus sp., herbivorous dinosaur. Jurassic. Simple, peg-like teeth. *(x ³/₅)*

Edentates

Edentates, meaning "toothless," were so named because anteaters and their kin have no teeth. All other edentates have teeth, but their teeth have no enamel and no roots.

The edentates first appeared in North America, then migrated to South America, where most of their evolutionary developments occurred. Some migrated back to North America during parts of the Miocene, Pliocene, and Pleistocene. This order includes armadillos, glyptodonts, ground sloths, tree sloths, and anteaters.

Armadillos

Two kinds of armadillos populated North America in the Pliocene and Pleistocene: *Dasypus bellus,* similar to the modern nine-banded armadillo but about twice its size, and *Holmesina,* the giant armadillo, which reached a length of about 7 feet and had three bands.

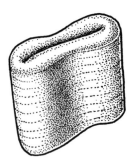

Holmesina sp., giant armadillo. Pleistocene.

Glyptodonts

Glyptodonts were bizarre animals that resembled mammals in tortoise shells. They evolved from early armadillos and developed outer shells of five- or six-sided bony plates that were joined together rigidly (armadillo armor is flexible) around the body. The head had a bony cap, and the tail was covered with bony rings.

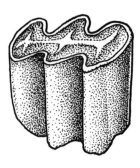

Glyptotherium sp., Pliocene to Pleistocene.

Ground Sloths

Ground sloths were a diverse group of hairy animals with different species occupying different ecological niches. All were herbivores.

Eremotherium **sp., giant ground sloth. Pliocene to Pleistocene. Largest land animal in North America (20 feet long). Teeth resemble double chisels; upper and lower molars are similar in appearance. This specimen is 9 inches long.** *(x ¹/₄)*

Megalonyx jeffersonii, **ground sloth. Pliocene to Pleistocene. The most widespread ground sloth in North America. Body was about the size of a cow. Canine tooth.** *(x ¹/₂)*

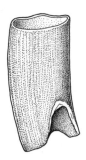

Paramylodon harlani, **ground sloth. Pliocene to Pleistocene. The most common ground sloth found at Rancho La Brea. Also known as** *Glossotherium harlani.* **Lower molar.** *(x ¹/₂)*

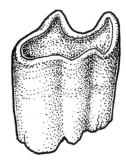

Saber-Toothed Cats

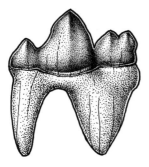

Smilodon **sp., saber-toothed cat. Pleistocene. Carnassial tooth, obviously designed for slicing.** $(x\,^3/_4)$

Capybaras

The capybara is the largest living rodent. It inhabits only South America today and is aquatic. The evolutionary history is not well understood, but capybaras reached North America in the Pliocene. The molars consist of plates of enamel.

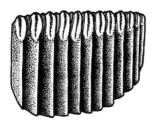

Neochoerus pinckneyi. **Pleistocene.** $(x\,^4/_5)$

Peccaries

Pigs and peccaries are closely related, but true pigs never reached North America (until introduced by European explorers and settlers), and peccaries filled their niche. The most common species of peccaries are *Mylohyus,* long-nosed forest dwellers, and *Platygonus,* which preferred open ground and may have lived in herds. Living species inhabit Central and South America and the American Southwest (javelinas).

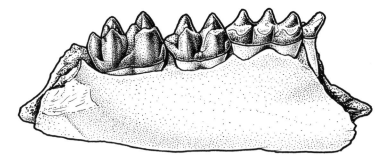

Platygonus sp. Pliocene to Pleistocene. Partial mandible.

Camels and Llamas

The mainstream of camel development occurred in North America until the Pliocene when they migrated to Asia. The first camels appeared in the Eocene of North America and were less than 2 feet tall. They bore little resemblance to present-day camels. Some camels also migrated to South America and evolved into llamas. Some llamas then returned to North America in the early Pleistocene. Camels became extinct in North America at the end of the Pleistocene.

Palaeolama sp., llama. Pleistocene. Upper molar.

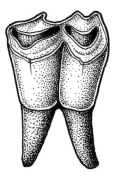

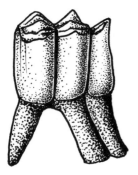

Palaeolama sp., llama. Pleistocene. Lower molar.

Deer

The first deer appeared about 25 million years ago in Asia. *Odocoileus virginianus*, the same species as the living white-tailed deer, first appeared in North America in the Pliocene, although it did not become common until the late Pleistocene. Like those of camels, llamas, and bison, cusps of deer teeth exhibit a crescent or selenodont shape.

Odocoileus virginianus, deer. Pleistocene. Upper molar. *(x 2)*

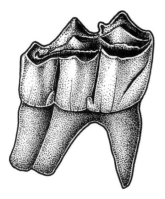

Odocoileus virginianus, deer. Pleistocene. Lower molar. *(x 2)*

Bison

The mainstream of evolutionary development of cattle and their kin took place in Eurasia and Africa. Bison reached North America about 1 million years ago, the only bovines to do so. Their success in terms of diversity of species and sheer numbers was remarkable. However, *Bison bison* is the only species of bison that has—just barely—survived extinction in North America. Bison molars are similar in shape to those of deer and camel, but they are typically much larger and are distinguished by the vertical stylid on the crown of the teeth.

Bison bison. **Pleistocene. Notice the isolated column. Upper molar.**

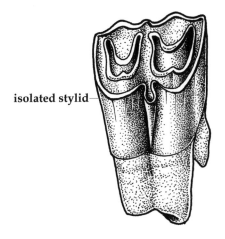

Bison antiquus. **Pleistocene. Notice the isolated column. Lower molar.**

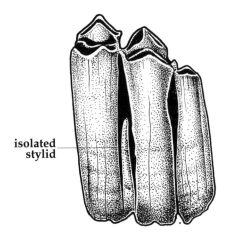

Horses

The first true horses appeared in the early Eocene in North America and Europe, although no one would mistake this 18-inch-tall animal as just a miniature version of the modern horse. *Hyracotherium* (also known as *Eohippus,* or dawn horse) had four toes on its forefeet and three toes on its hind feet. It had low-crowned teeth and was a forest dweller.

The evolutionary history of horses leading to the modern species took place in North America. It has been well documented and includes the trends of increasing size, fewer toes, and higher-crowned (taller) teeth. The genus *Equus,* which includes the modern horse, first appeared in the late Pliocene and survived until the end of the Pleistocene in North America. *Equus* was reintroduced into the Americas by European explorers.

The hipparion type of horse was a branch that was separate from the line that led to *Equus.* The hipparions were a slender, gracile form that became extinct in the Pliocene. Their upper molars are distinguished by an isolated protocone in the enamel. Horses were very successful in North America. A recent cataloging of species indicates that more than fifty different species, from the Oligocene to the Pleistocene, have been found in Florida alone. Not all may be valid, but the number is amazing.

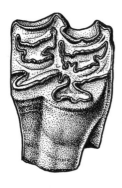

Equus **sp., one-toed horse. Pliocene to Pleistocene. Upper molar.** *(x $^9/_{10}$)*

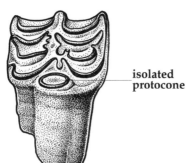

isolated protocone

Hipparion-type, three-toed horse. Miocene to Pliocene. Gazellelike animal. Teeth are distinguished by an isolated protocone, the circular ridge of enamel evident on the chewing surface. Upper molar. *(x $^9/_{10}$)*

Equus sp. Lower molar.

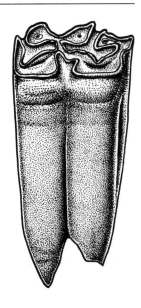

Equus sp. Incisor.

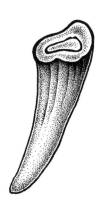

Tapirs

Tapirs are closely related to rhinoceroses and first appeared at about the same time. Tapirs did not exhibit the same kind of diversity over time, but they do last longer in the fossil record. Pleistocene tapirs were abundant in North America, although living species are restricted to South America and Southeast Asia.

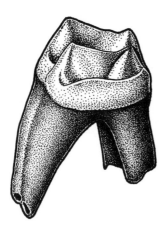

Tapirus veroensis. **Pliocene to Pleistocene. Upper molar.**

Rhinoceroses

Rhinoceroses have a long, rich history in North America, first appearing in the Eocene and later spreading to the rest of the world. By the Oligocene, they exhibited three body types: a St. Bernard–size upland dweller with slim legs and long, three-toed feet, called *Hyracodon;* the "running rhino," an aquatic, hippopotamuslike rhino with short, stocky legs and broad feet, called *Metamynodon;* and the lowland body type of living rhinos, called *Caenopus.* In the Miocene and Pliocene, *Teleoceras,* a hippolike but true rhino, was abundant across North America. Rhinoceroses became extinct in North America during the Pliocene. Interestingly, the largest known land mammal was the Asian rhino, *Indricotherium,* which stood nearly 20 feet tall at the shoulder.

From the earliest species to living species, rhino molars and premolars, except for size, have changed very little and are quite distinctive.

Teleoceras sp., true rhino. Pliocene. Upper molar. *(x ³/₄)*

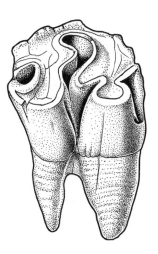

Hyracodon nebrascensis, "running rhino." Oligocene. Lower molar. *(x 1¹/₂)*

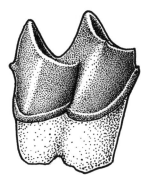

Elephants

Fossils of the earliest known ancestors of elephants come from Eocene formations in Egypt about 55 million years old, and nearly 140 other species have been described in the fossil record since that time. The African *(Loxodonta africana)* and Asian *(Elephas maximus)* elephants are the only two living species. The closest living relatives of the elephants are hyraxes (described as overgrown guinea pigs) and sirenians, or sea cows, which include manatees and dugongs.

Elephantlike animals reached North America during the Miocene, but the evolutionary developments here were not part of the lineage leading to living species. The first elephantlike stock reached North America about 15 million years ago. They belonged to a group known as gomphotheres, a rather nonspecific grouping of North American elephants including *Gomphotherium,* a long-jawed four-tusker; *Amebelodon,* a very long-jawed "shovel-tusker"; and *Cuvieronius,* a short-jawed two-tusker. The mastodon, *Mammut americanum,* belonged to a related family.

Mammoths migrated to North America in the earliest part of the Pleistocene. The first mammoths to arrive in North America belonged to the species *Mammuthus meridionalis. Mammuthus columbi,* the Columbian mammoth, was its descendant in North America, and *Mammuthus primigenius,* the woolly mammoth, was its descendant in Europe and Asia. About 100,000 years ago, the woolly mammoth also migrated across a land bridge to North America. All three groups survived until the end of the Pleistocene. Evidence suggests that several dwarf species survived on isolated islands off the coasts of California and Siberia until as recently as 4,000 years ago.

Elephants were plentiful in North America, and their fossils have been found in many states. Interestingly, elephant fossils have been found in every county in Nebraska. Not surprisingly, the mammoth is the state fossil of Nebraska.

The most common elephant fossil finds are their teeth and pieces of tusk, or ivory. Their bones were generally porous and not well preserved. Infant premolars of elephants may be only 1 inch long; the sixth tooth of an adult can be a foot long.

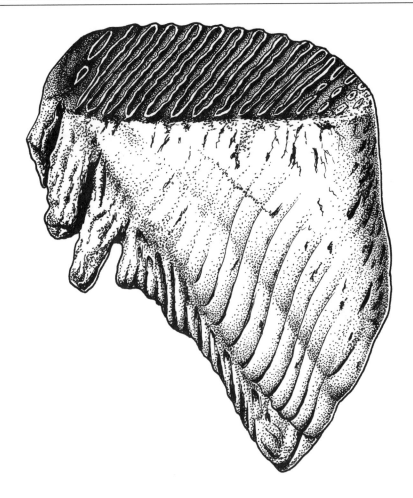

Mammuthus primigenius, **woolly mammoth. Pleistocene. Mammoth teeth are composed of plates of enamel separated from each other and held together by dentine and cement. All three components wore at different rates, resulting in a washboard effect. Mammoths were grazers and fed on grasses, sedges, and shrubs. Only a small part of the tooth extended above the gum. As teeth became worn, they moved forward in the jaw and up or down in the mandible or maxilla, respectively. Complete teeth are found, although individual plates or partial teeth are more frequent finds. (x $^{1}/_{3}$)**

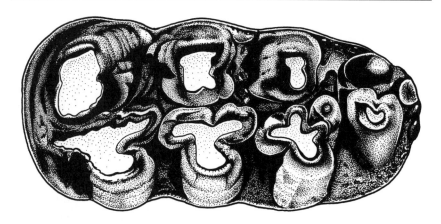

Gomphothere (species unknown). Miocene to Pleistocene. Gomphothere teeth have an enamel crown with complex patterns of cones
arranged in transverse rows, with smaller conules at the front and in
the valleys between the larger cones. Adult teeth, as in this specimen, show differential wear from one side of the tooth to the other
and a distinctive trefoil pattern. A forest dweller and a browser, the
gomphothere had teeth designed for mashing leaves and branches.
Complete teeth with crowns and roots are found, although partial
teeth are more common finds. Dorsal view. *(x ⁹/₁₀)*

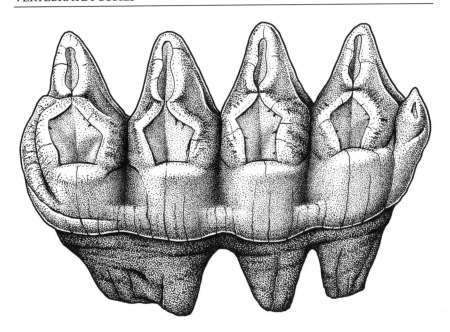

Mammut americanum, mastodon. Pleistocene. Mastodon teeth exhibit a simple pattern of cones arranged to form transverse ridges with open valleys between them. Adult teeth show differential wear from one side of the tooth to the other but do not exhibit a trefoil pattern. This specimen is very worn. Mastodons were forest dwellers. Dorsal/lateral view. *(x ⁹/₁₀)*

Tusks are greatly enlarged incisors that have shed their enamel and are composed of dentine. Complete lengths of tusks are very rare finds. Typically, a cross section will reveal a distinctive cross-hatching pattern. More frequently, pieces or flakes of tusk are found. They are usually mistaken for petrified wood, as the growth rings of the ivory appear similar to the growth rings of trees. Fossilized ivory will generally feel silky smooth, and individual pieces may exhibit the distinctive cross-hatching.

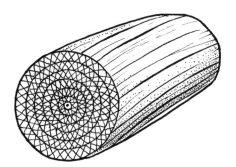

Tusk/ivory. Cross section. *(x ¹/₄)*

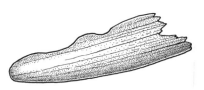

Tusk. Partial tusk including tip. *(x 1¹/₄)*

Sirenians (Sea Cows)

Sirenians include dugongs, manatees, and their kin. They have been found from the Eocene to the present and are distantly related to elephants, having split off from a common ancestor about 55 to 65 million years ago.

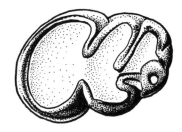

Metaxytherium floridanum, dugong. Miocene. Several species dominated Western Hemisphere tropical waters during the Miocene and Pliocene. The dugong disappeared from the Western Hemisphere about 2 to 3 million years ago, when the isthmus of Central America was completed. The living species is a saltwater dweller that inhabits only Indopacific waters. It is best distinguished by its whale-like tail. Dorsal view (chewing surface heavily worn).

Trichechus manatus, West Indian manatee. Pleistocene to recent. It first evolved in South American rivers but appeared in Caribbean and North American waters about the time the isthmus of Central America was complete. Single tooth with small amount of root showing. *(x 1¹/₂)*

Desmostylians

Desmostylians were Pacific coast inhabitants of North America and Asia. The skull is horselike, the body is something of a cross between a walrus and a hippo, and the molar teeth are unique among mammals. Each molar is composed of columns of dentine surrounded by thick enamel.

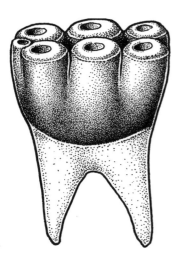

Desmostylus **sp. Miocene. Unique teeth forming clusters of upright cylinders. Lower molar.**

Whales and Dolphins

Whales evolved from terrestrial, carnivorous scavengers, called mesonychids, in the early Eocene. Recent finds in Pakistan demonstrate the evolution from fully terrestrial wolf-size animals, through numerous intermediate forms, to fully marine animals.

By the mid-Eocene, archaeocete whales such as *Zygorhiza* (the state fossil of Mississippi) and the serpentlike *Basilosaurus* (the state fossil of Alabama) reached lengths of 50 and 30 feet, respectively. They retained the dentition of their terrestrial ancestors, with sharp, conical teeth in the front of the jaw and serrated, bladelike teeth in the back. The archaeocete whales declined during the Oligocene and were gone by the Miocene.

The archaeocetes led to the more modern, toothed (odontocete) and baleen (mysticete) whales, as well as true dolphins and porpoises, which first appeared in the Miocene. The teeth of odontocetes differ from the archaeocetes in that all of their teeth are of the sharp, conical form and show little variation in the jaw. *Squalodon*, the archaeocetelike, "shark-toothed porpoise," became extinct by the end of the Miocene.

Squalodon   *Zygorhiza*

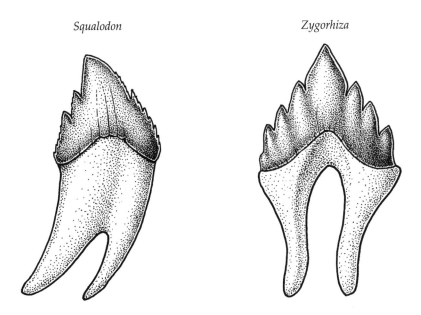

Squalodon **sp./***Zygorhiza* **sp., The teeth of archaeocete whales and squalodons are similar and can be mistaken for each other. Generally,** *Squalodon* **is a Miocene find and** *Zygorhiza* **is an Eocene find, but mixed sediments do occur. Thus, it is the extent of the notch in the root that distinguishes them. Also, the maximum size of archaeocete teeth is significantly larger than that of squalodons. (*x 1*, *³/₄, respectively*)**

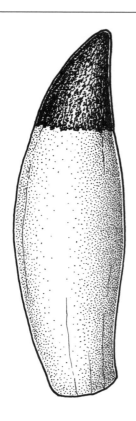 

Physeter **sp., sperm whale. Miocene to Recent. Teeth have enamel at the tip only. Thinner specimen shows growth rings.** *(x ¹/₂)*

Kentriodon **sp., dolphin. Mio-cene.**

Section 1B • *Vertebrae*

The vertebral column, or spine, provides support for the body and protection for the spinal cord. It is composed of individual bones, called vertebrae (singular: vertebra), separated, in life, by cartilaginous intervertebral disks. Vertebrae are usually made of bone and fossilize easily, whereas the disks do not. However, the vertebrae of sharks, rays, and skates are composed of cartilage (not bone) that usually does not fossilize. The actual number of vertebrae in living species ranges from nine in frogs to upward of four hundred in snakes. Most vertebrae can be identified as to the family and position in the spinal column, but species identification is usually not possible.

The shapes of vertebrae differ dramatically both within an individual animal, depending on their position in the spinal column, and across species as well. Almost all vertebrae share the characteristics seen in the whale/dolphin lumbar vertebra.

The main portion of a vertebra is the body, or centrum. Just above the centrum is an opening, the vertebral foramen or neural canal, through

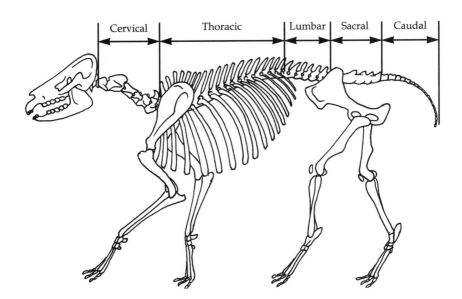

Figure 11.1. Vertebrae positions.

which the spinal cord passes. The size of the opening is indicative of the position in the spinal column. The spinal cord is thickest as it leaves the skull and tapers toward the end of the body, as does the size of the vertebral foramen. Above the vertebral foramen is a vertical, bony projection called the spinous process. To the sides of the centrum are lateral projections called transverse processes. The main function of the spinous and transverse processes is to provide attachments for muscles. Their size and shape also vary within an individual, depending on their position in the spinal column. The majority of fossil vertebrae consist of centra only, as the processes break off easily.

Mammalian vertebrae are grouped based on their position in the spinal column. Cervical vertebrae are positioned from just behind the skull until the ribs. The first vertebra behind the skull is called the atlas and is usually cupped to fit the back of the skull. The second vertebra is called the axis, which usually has a portion of its centrum projecting into the atlas in front of it. These unique shapes allow for the head to nod and swivel. The rest of the cervical vertebrae support the neck and exhibit structures called transverse foramina (singular: foramen), which protect cranial blood vessels. Only cervical vertebrae exhibit them, but they may be missing in fossil finds due to breakage.

The thoracic vertebrae articulate with the ribs. In well-preserved specimens, the point of articulation with the ribs can be observed as a pair of small indentations near the top of the centrum. Thoracic vertebrae are characterized by tall spinous processes, which provide attachment for the back and shoulder muscles.

The lumbar vertebrae occupy the position between the ribs and the sacrum or pelvis. Lumbar vertebrae are characterized by long transverse processes, which provide attachment for back muscles.

The sacral vertebrae usually fuse into a single structure called the sacrum, which fits snugly into the pelvis. Complete specimens are quite rare, as the sacrum readily breaks into irregular pieces.

Caudal vertebrae compose the bony structure of the tail. They are usually quite small and nondescript, and are uncommon finds. The rarity may be due in part to the fact that collectors are generally looking for bigger, more recognizable vertebrae.

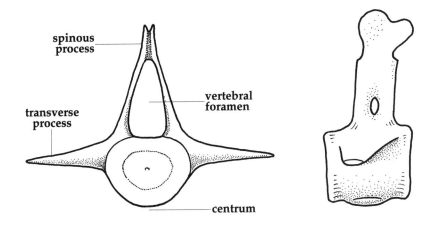

Whale/dolphin. Lumbar vertebra. *(x ⁴/₅)*

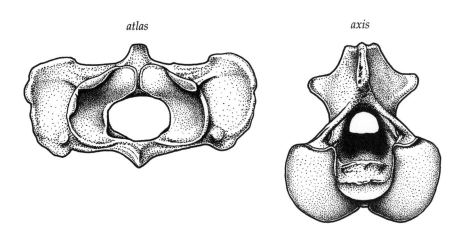

Equus **sp. Representative land animal vertebrae.** *(x ¹/₂)*

cervical   *thoracic*

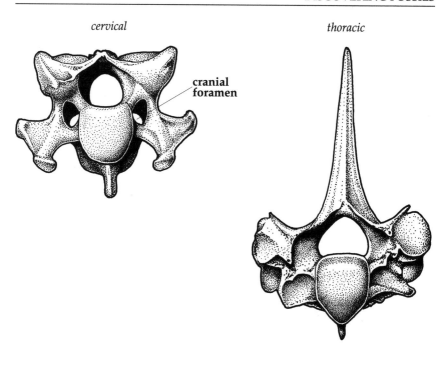

cranial
foramen

lumbar

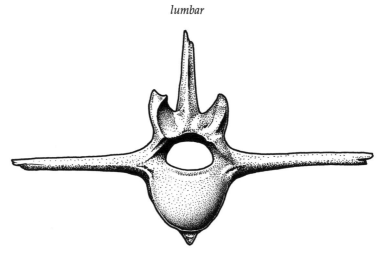

Equus **sp. Representative land animal vertebrae.** *(Cervical vertebrae x ¹/₂)*

Oreodont (species unknown). Caudal vertebra, tailbone. *(x 1¹/₂)*

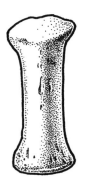

Metaxytherium **sp., dugong. Sea cow thoracic vertebrae are noted for being heart shaped, as are some elephant vertebrae.** *(x ⁴/₅)*

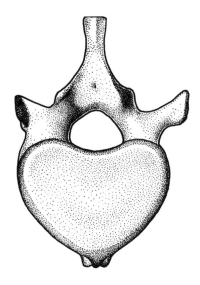

Alligator mississippiensis. **Note ball and socket joint and rough appearance on anterior end.** *(x ⁴/₅)*

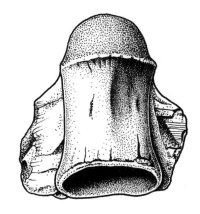

Snake (species unknown). Reptilian ball and socket joint, posterior view. *(x 3)*

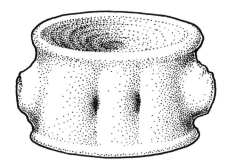

Plesiosaur (species unknown). Slightly concave on both sides. *(x ³/₁₀)*

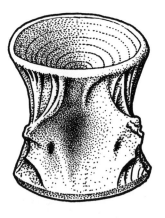

Fish (species unknown). Almost all bony fish vertebrae are concave at both ends.

Fish (species unknown). "Swollen," looks like rattlesnake rattle. *(x 1¹/₄)*

Fish, filefish. *(x 1¹/₁₀)*

Fish, hake.

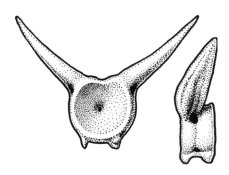

Shark. All shark, ray, and skate vertebrae are concave on both ends. Lamnoid-type centrum.

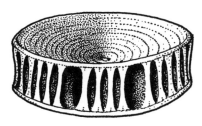

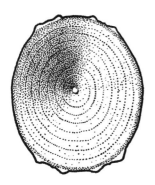

Shark. Scyliorhinoid-type centrum. Top view.

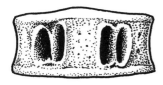

Shark. Scyliorhinoid-type centrum. Side view.

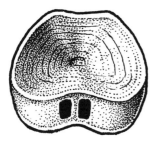

Batoid. Ray or skate vertebra.

Section 1C • Bones

Unless you have found a complete fossilized bone, the most obvious indicator is its "spongy" appearance. The next time you eat a T-bone steak, examine the bone and you will see why this description is accurate. Note that there is a smooth outside layer, called the cortex, and spongy-looking material inside, called the medulla, where the marrow is present.

One frustrating aspect of vertebrate fossil collecting concerns identification. You may leaf through scientific texts and see photographs of totally unrecognizable (to you) fragments of bone or teeth being described down to the subspecies and which side of the animal it came from. Yet, when you take a well-preserved piece of bone with distinguishing aspects to an expert, you are told, "Well, it might be a piece of a limb bone from a herbivore." So be prepared for some disappointment, as most bone finds are unidentifiable unless they are complete or include a proximal or distal end.

Here are some rules of thumb for identifying bones:

• Modern-type whale and dolphin bones tend to have a thin layer of cortex.

• Bird bones have a thin cortex that is described as "raspy" or "flaky." They are generally hollow or have thin, bony internal struts. Not all hollow bones are bird bones, however, because the medulla may have degraded before fossilization occurred.

• Reptilian bones also have a thin cortex and may be hollow. (Given a probable common ancestor with birds, this is not surprising.) Reptilian bones frequently exhibit a rough, worn appearance on the proximal and distal ends. This is because they do not have epiphyses. (See description of juvenile bones in Section 1E.)

• Sloth bones tend to have a cortex that appears arthritic or pathological and has been described as looking like shredded wheat. In fact, that is the normal condition.

• Some bones are extremely dense with no medulla. These include the tympanic bulla (ear bone) of marine mammals, the astragalus (anklebone) of land animals, and most sea cow bones.

• Many bones are variations on a theme. For example, once you see the "cutout" of a proximal ulna (the elbow in humans) you will always know it. For toe bones, a rounded end with a dimple on both sides of the distal end is a dead giveaway. You may not know what species your find is, but chances are an expert can identify what family it belongs to.

• Some bones from different parts of the body appear similar. The proximal humerus (shoulder) and the proximal femur (hip) appear very similar. Both are parts of ball-and-socket joints. Since they perform similar functions, similar form is to be expected. However, the proximal femur is distinguished from the humerus in that it is more round, is connected by a longer neck to the main shaft of the bone, and has a small indentation or groove on the ball.

• Generally speaking, stout limb bones are indicative of slow-moving herbivores. Graceful bones with sharply defined angles for muscle attachments are indicative of carnivores.

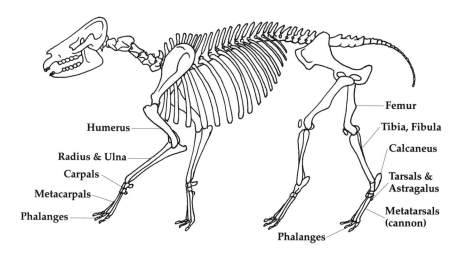

Figure 11.2. Limb bones.

LIMB BONES

Front Leg

From the distal end, the front leg consists of hooves or claws, a series of two phalanges or toe bones (which make up an individual digit), metacarpals (which are longer than phalanges), carpals (wrist bones), two lower leg/arm bones (radius and ulna), and one upper leg/arm bone (humerus), which articulates with the shoulder blade. The proximal ulna usually exhibits a very distinctive curved cutout shape, which helps it articulate with the humerus (at the elbow in humans). In some animals, such as the horse or sea cow, the radius and ulna are either partially or completely fused.

Back Leg

From the distal end, the hind leg consists of hooves or claws, two phalanges, metatarsals, tarsals (which include the anklebones), two lower leg or shin bones (tibia and fibula), and an upper leg or thigh bone (femur), which articulates with the pelvis. Some animals have a fused tibia and fibula (horse). Even-toed, hoofed animals (artiodactyls) have fused metatarsal bones called cannon bones.

It is most unusual to find a complete limb bone, so only proximal and distal ends are presented here. Some ends of bones are far more obvious than others. For this reason, only easily recognizable ends are included. The specimens presented are typical forms that are representative of a wide variety of species, genera, and families. Unless you choose to study comparative skeletal anatomy, actual species identification may be difficult, but the size of the fossil and its site location will help narrow the choices. In the end, it takes an expert to recognize the subtle differences among species.

Oreodonts were common ruminant artiodactyls of the Oligocene and Miocene of North America only, some of which survived to the Pliocene. They were pig- or sheeplike animals whose fossils are abundant in the Big Badlands of South Dakota and Nebraska. Most were browsers, but some species were tree climbers and some were semiaquatic. Their bones are presented here as representatives of proximal and distal limb bones.

proximal humerus   *proximal femur*

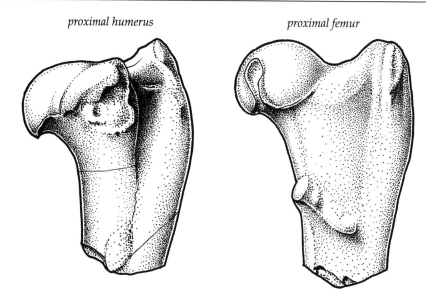

Oreodont (species unknown). Oligocene. Proximal humerus articulates with scapula to form shoulder. The ball is a flattened circle that is close to the shaft of the bone. Proximal femur articulates with pelvis to form hip. The ball is round, exhibits a dimple or groove, and is extended farther from the shaft of the bone.

side view   *posterior view*

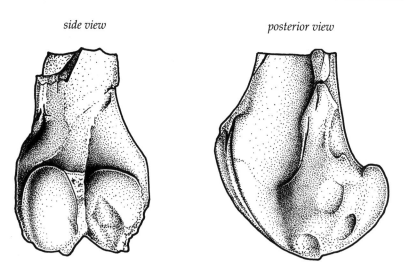

Oreodont (species unknown). Oligocene. Distal femur. Articulates with proximal shin bones and kneecap to form the knee joint.

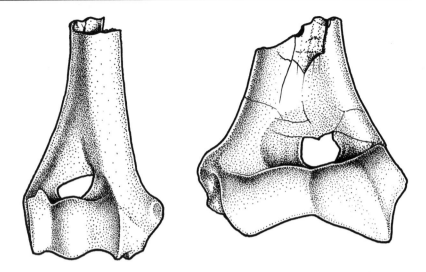

Oreodont (species unknown) and saber-toothed cat (species unknown). Oligocene. Herbivore and carnivore, respectively. Distal humerus. In oreodonts, the area of bone just above the articulating
surface is usually quite thin, so many fossil finds exhibit a hole. In
saber-toothed cats, the articulating surface is wider than that of the
oreodonts and has more sharply defined ridges, allowing for a wider
range of limb movement.

posterior view   *anterior view*

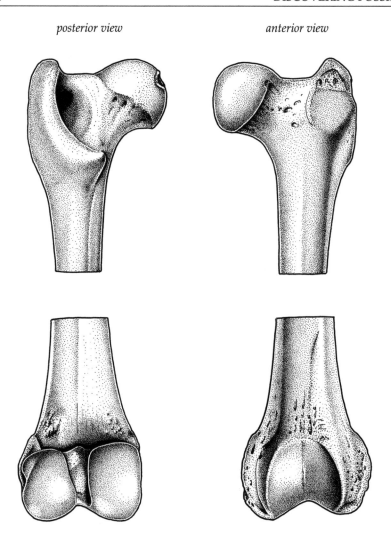

Smilodon gracilis. **Saber-toothed cat. Pleistocene. This animal was a fearsome predator, and its leg bone exhibits all the subtle features that gave the animal its flexibility and strength. Proximal and distal femur, front and back views.** *(x ³/₈)*

Saber-toothed cat (species unknown). Oligocene. Carnivore.
Proximal ulna. Distinguishing
feature is the cutout or scallop
that helps form the elbow (in
humans). (x $^3/_4$)

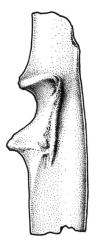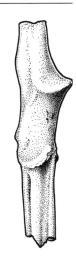

Oreodont (species unknown). Oligocene. Herbivore. Distal tibia.
Distinguishing feature is the projection of bone. (x $1^1/_2$)

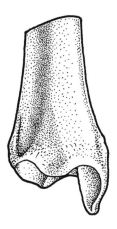

FEET

These figures (following pages) illustrate the difference between the foot
bones of odd-toed (perissodactyls) and even-toed (artiodactyls) hoofed
animals. In life, the hoof consists of a bony core covered by keratin. The
keratin rarely fossilizes. These animals actually walked on the tips of
their toes.

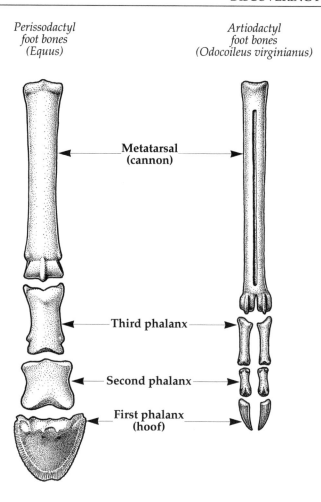

*Perissodactyl
foot bones
(Equus)*

*Artiodactyl
foot bones
(Odocoileus virginianus)*

Metatarsal
(cannon)

Third phalanx

Second phalanx

First phalanx
(hoof)

Equus sp., horse, and *Odocoileus virginianus,* white-tailed deer. Pleistocene. *Equus* exhibits one toe (actually its third toe), consisting of a series of four bones: three phalanges and a long metacarpal or metatarsal. *Odocoileus virginianus* exhibits two toes (actually its third and fourth toes), consisting of three pairs of phalanges and one long metatarsal that is actually two metatarsals that are fused. This fused metatarsal is unique to artiodactyls and is called a cannon bone. The groove in the cannon bone and the narrow separation of the distal ends are indicative of deer and bison cannon bones. $(x\,^{7}/_{10})$

Hemiauchenia sp., llama. Pliocene to Pleistocene. Distal end
of cannon bone is splayed, typical of camels as well. No groove
in cannon bone. *(x ³/₈)*

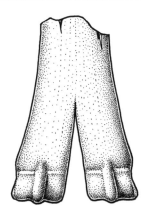

TOES

Toe bones are easily recognizable from their characteristic ends. One end
is rounded, with a dimple on each side; the other is curved so that it articulates with the rounded end of the bone behind it.

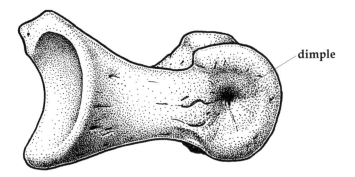

dimple

Sloth (species unknown). Short for its overall size, sturdy, and robust.

Small carnivore (species unknown). Long and slender.

ANKLEBONE, OR ASTRAGALUS

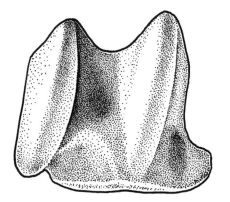

Mesohippus sp., horse. Oligocene. Exhibits the "single pulley" form common among perissodactyls.

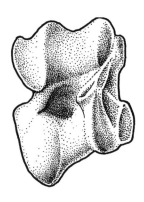

Oreodont (species unknown). Oligocene. Exhibits the "double pulley" form common among artiodactyls. *(x 1¹/₂)*

HEEL

Achilles tendon

Achilles tendon

 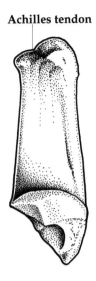

Odocoileus virginianus, deer. Pleistocene. Calcaneus (heel). This general form is very common among extinct and living animals. The Achilles tendon fits into the groove at the distal end. Frontal view and side view. *(x ⁴/₅)*

BIRD BONES

Though the earliest evolution of birds is a matter of conjecture, the fossils of unequivocal birds appear in the Jurassic. Because of their delicate structure, bird fossils are rare. As the cutaway drawing illustrates, most bird bones have a thin cortex and are either hollow or have struts that provide support. The outside and ends of bird and reptilian bones are described as raspy or flaky. The ends of the bones have no cortex because they have no epiphyses.

Given the delicate nature of bird bones, it is rare to find even fragments, much less complete bones. Although all hollow bones should be investigated, not all hollow bones are bird bones. Fossil mammal bones may appear hollow because the medulla sometimes disintegrates before fossilization, and, in fact, some parts of them are hollow.

All modern birds have three bones that are unlike any others found in the animal world: the coracoid, carpometacarpus, and tarsometatarsus.

Each species may show a variation on the theme, but for the most part, they are comparable among most birds.

Don't assume all bird bones are small; *Titanis walleri* stood nearly 10 feet tall, and *Teratornis* had a wingspan of nearly 20 feet.

The accompanying illustrations of complete bird bones are specimens from an as-yet-unnamed Pliocene cormorantlike bird.

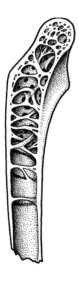

Bird bone. Cutaway showing bony struts. *(x $^4/_5$)*

Coracoid. Articulates with shoulder blade and braces wing against the breastbone. *(x $^{4.5}/_5$)*

Carpometacarpus. Fused carpal and metacarpal bones found in the wing tip. *(x ⁴·⁵/₅)*

Tarsometatarsus. Fused tarsal and metatarsal bones; articulates with toe bones. *(x ⁴·⁵/₅)*

CLAWS

Claws consist of a bony core covered by keratin. The keratin rarely fossilizes, so claws of living specimens are bigger than fossilized claws, which are more correctly identified as claw cores.

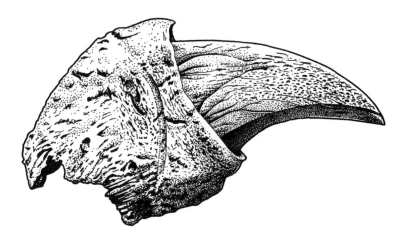

Eremotherium **sp., giant ground sloth. Pleistocene. This specimen is 23 inches long.** *(x ³/₁₆)*

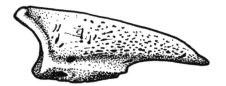

Holmesina floridanum, **giant armadillo. Pleistocene.**

ANTLERS

Antlers are frontal bone outgrowths that are periodically shed and grown again. In life, they are covered by vascular "velvet" during active growth. Antler is similar in structure to bone, with a hard, compact cortex and "spongy" medulla. Horns consist of a bony core encased in a horny sheath that is an agglutinated hair structure. The bony cores of horns fossilize, but the sheath usually does not.

Odocoileus virginianus, **deer. Pleistocene. Piece of antler.**

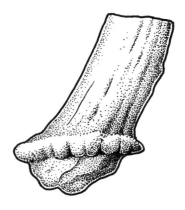

MISCELLANEOUS BONES

Sarda **sp., bonita. Fish "nose," dorsal and posterior views. (x 1³/₄)**

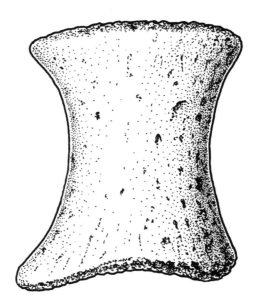

Whale (species unknown). Phalanx (finger bone).

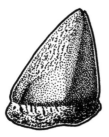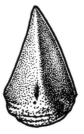

Tortoise. May be mistaken for a claw, but is too stubby. Leg spur.

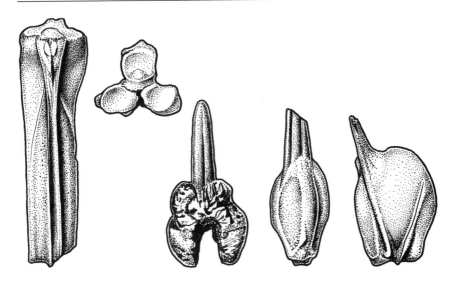

Fish (species unknown). Ballast or bladder bones. These odd-shaped bones grow on the vertebrae of fish. Their purpose and function are unknown. They come in a variety of sizes and shapes and are frequently mistaken for other kinds of bones.

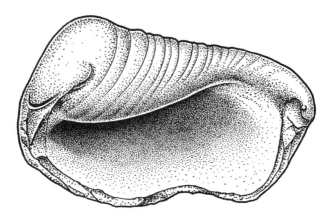

Whale/dolphin. One of the ear bones, exceptionally dense and solid. Tympanic bulla.

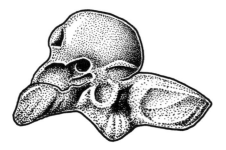

Dolphin. Another ear bone. Periotic bone. *(x 2)*

Ray. Tail spine or stinger. Barb.

Catfish. Spine.

Shark. Shark cartilage sometimes does fossilize. It has a
very distinctive surface texture.
Calcified cartilage. *(x 1¹/₂)*

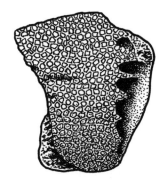

Section 1D • Shells, Scutes, and Scales

SHELLS

Turtles and tortoises first appeared in the Triassic, having evolved from reptiles. Pieces of their shells are by far the most common remains and can be indicative of the type of turtle, although not the species.

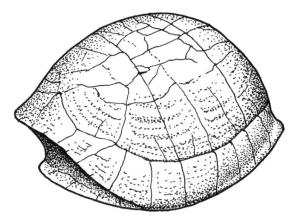

Stylemys **sp. Oligocene. Very common in the Badlands of South Dakota and Nebraska. Complete tortoise shell.** *(x ¹/₄)*

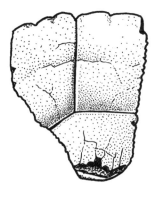

Pseudemys **sp., pond turtle. Pleistocene. Shell fragment.**

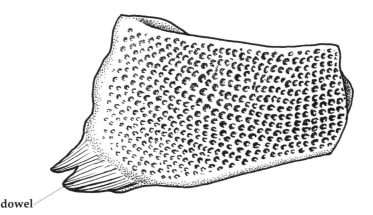

dowel

Trionyx sp., softshell turtle. Cretaceous to recent. Shell fragment with "dowel" that fits into adjacent plate. Note how the texture differs from other specimens.

SCUTES

Scutes, also called osteoderms, are individual plates of bony armor.

Alligator mississippiensis, **American alligator. The alligator's scute can be distinguished from that of the crocodile, which tends to be rounder and does not exhibit the raised medial ridge. Scute.**

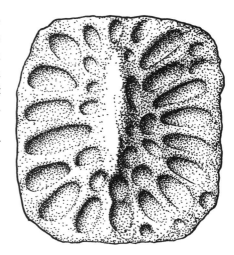

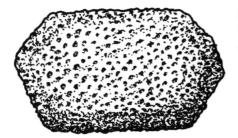

Holmesina sp., giant armadillo. Scute.

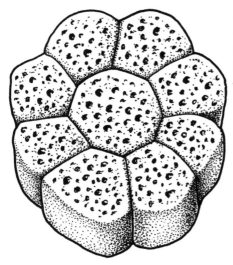

Glyptotherium sp., glyptodont. Flower-shaped scutes formed a shell that covered nearly the entire body. Scute.

SCALES

Ray (species unknown). Miocene. Found on dorsal surface
of body and tail. Dermal scales.

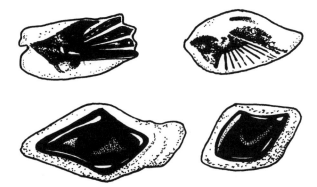

Garfish. Cretaceous to recent. These scales have an enamel-like surface. Scales.

Section 1E • Oddities

PATHOLOGICAL SPECIMENS

Just as in life today, animals of the past sometimes suffered from pathological conditions. It is especially rewarding—and valuable—to find fossils with such evidence.

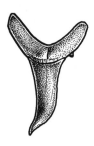
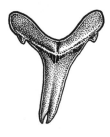

Carcharias taurus, **sand tiger.
Two teeth with common path-
ologies, a bent crown and a
split crown. Shark teeth.** *(x 1¹/₂)*

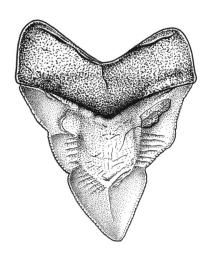

The *Carcharocles megalodon* **tooth is self-evident. Shark tooth.** *(x ³/₄)*

This distal femur was broken in life and also suffered an infection. Broken bone. *(x ²/₃)*

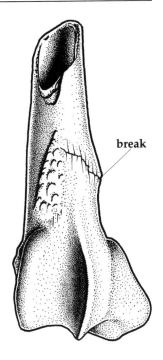

break

Oreodont. This astragalus and calcaneus were fused in life. Fused bones. *(x 1¹/₂)*

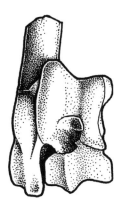

JUVENILE SPECIMENS

Many mammalian bones do not grow from their extreme ends, but from a region of the shaft just behind it. Thus, a juvenile bone consists of a main shaft and two epiphyses that cap it on each end. A thin layer of cartilage, the epiphyseal plate, or growth plate, joins the cap to the shaft. New bone grows in this thin plate, which then extends the shaft. When growth ceases, the epiphyses fuse to the shaft. Depending on the developmental stage of the animal, epiphyses may or may not stay attached to the fossilized bone.

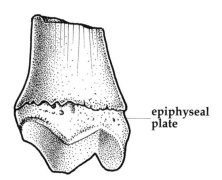

epiphyseal plate

Oreodont. The epiphysis on this distal tibia has not fused entirely with the main shaft of the bone. Therefore, the animal was a juvenile when it died. Distal tibia.

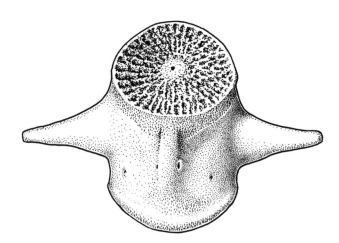

Dolphin. Here, the epiphysis separated from the centrum after the animal died but before fossilization. Vertebra. *(x ³/₄)*

UNERUPTED OR RECENTLY ERUPTED TEETH

Unerupted or recently erupted mammalian teeth usually look quite different than worn teeth from mature adults.

chewing surface   *lateral view*

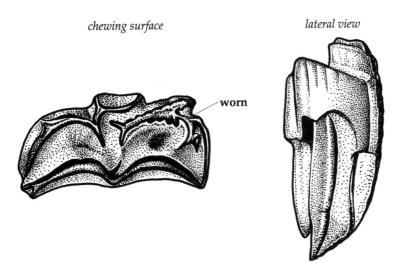

worn

Equus **sp., horse. Lower molar. This recently erupted tooth looks different from an adult tooth. Note that this tooth has seen some use, as the complex enamel pattern seen in adults is starting to become evident in this view of the chewing surface.**

12

Evidence of Activity

COPROLITES

Coprolites are feces that have become fossilized through the deposition of minerals. They are common, yet they often go uncollected because most exhibit a nondistinct shape. Shark coprolites exhibit a distinctive pattern produced by the structure of the lower intestine. In general, if it looks like what you think it is, it probably is; but kick it with your boot to be sure it's a fossil before you pick it up. Connoisseurs of coprolites treasure specimens with pieces of bones, teeth, or fish scales evident.

Mammalian coprolite.

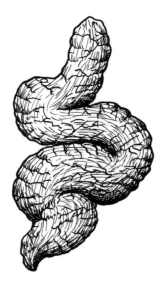

Shark coprolite.

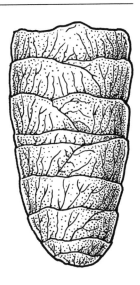

BITE MARKS

Check pieces of whale, dolphin, seal, and sea cow bones for parallel groups of scratches or gouges. These marks are indicative of predation by a shark's multiple rows of teeth. Occasionally, a piece of a tooth will stay embedded in the bone.

Less common are compression bite marks from terrestrial and marine carnivores. Look carefully for several evenly spaced and evenly formed indentations. They may match up with pairs of canines of terrestrial carnivores or rows of teeth from alligators, mosasaurs, or other marine reptiles.

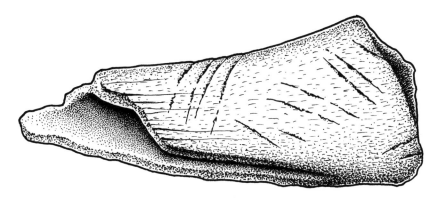

Shark. Whale bone with shark tooth marks.

Carnivore. Antler with carnivore bite marks.

TRACKS, TRAILS, AND BURROWS

Most fossils are the remains of animals that have died. Tracks, trails, and burrows differ in that they are the remains of living animals. For this reason, they hold a special place in the hearts and minds of some collectors.

The frustrating aspect of track identification is that they lend themselves, in most cases, to only a rough guess of what animal left them. Trails can be better identified, especially if the animal dies at the end of it. Burrows also may have their makers fossilized in them, making identification easier.

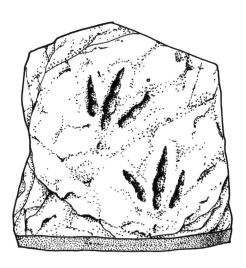

Anomoepus crassus, **theropod dinosaur. Jurassic. Tracks.** *(x 1/4)*

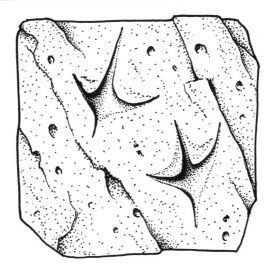

Bird (species unknown). Eocene. Tracks. *(x 1¹/₂)*

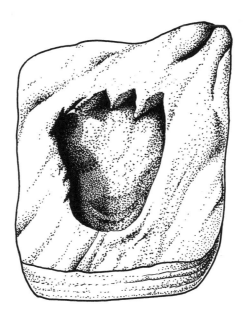

Apatosaurus **sp., sauropod dinosaur. Cretaceous. Track.** *(x ¹/₂₀)*

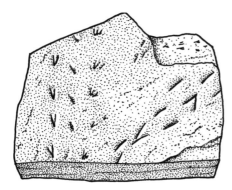

Insect (species unknown). Permian. Two regular rows of marks that may touch each other to form two continuous parallel lines. Trail. $(x\ 1^7/_{10})$

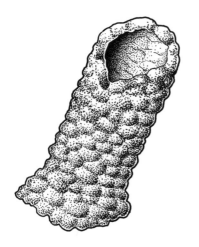

Ophiomorpha nodosa, ghost shrimp. Cretaceous to Pleistocene. Burrow. $(x\ ^3/_4)$

13

Plant Fossils

LYCOPODS

Lycopods, commonly called club mosses, are the most primitive trees. They first appeared in the Devonian and were dominant in the Carboniferous, and there are living species today. Most coal is made of their leaves, stems, and trunks.

Lepidodendron **sp., lycopod. Pennsylvanian to Permian. The most common lycopod fossil. Leaves grew on the trunk, and the diamond-shaped structures arranged in diagonal rows were the leaf cushions. These plants grew up to 100 feet tall.** (*x* ³/₄)

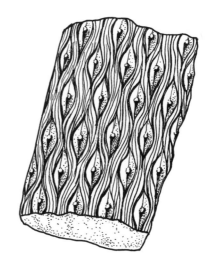

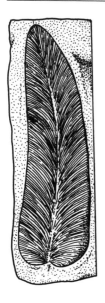

Neuropteris scheuchzeri, seed fern. Pennsylvanian. Common in North America. These were fernlike plants that produced seeds. Leaflets (pinnules) attached to the leaf stalk at a single point. Flowering plants may have evolved from seed ferns. $(x\ ^3/_4)$

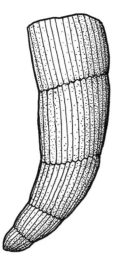

Calamites sp., horsetail. Pennsylvanian to Permian. Grew as tall as 40 feet. Most fossil specimens are molds of the pith, stems, and branches.

Annularia stellata. Pennsylvanian. Given a separate name before being recognized as having come from *Calamites.* Flower-shaped leaf whorls. *(x ⁴/₅)*

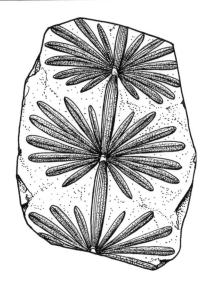

CYCADS

Cycads lived from the Triassic to the present. They probably evolved from seed ferns. Cycads typically have short, squat trunks that do not branch and a crown of large, palmlike leaves. Seeds are borne in cones.

Cycadeoidea marylandica, cycad. Cretaceous. The plant's trunk was similar in appearance to that of the unrelated pineapple. Fronds rose out of the top. Triangular scars were leaf cushions. *(x ¹/₁₀)*

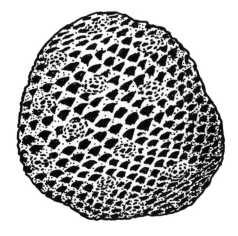

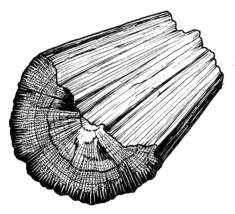

Petrified wood. Triassic to Pleistocene. The best specimens look just like wood. *(x $^9/_{10}$)*

14

Invertebrate Fossils

CORALS

Astrhelia palmata, coral. Miocene. Non-reef-building, colonial, and branching. Small, round calices evenly separated.

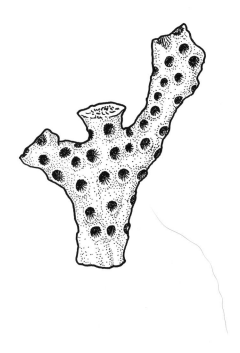

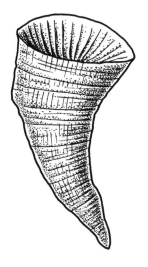

Pseudozaphrentoides **sp., rugose or horn coral. Pennsylvanian. Noncolonial.**

BRACHIOPODS

Brachiopods truly fit the description of living fossils in that they first appeared in the Cambrian and nearly three hundred species are alive today. More than twelve thousand fossil species are known. Brachiopods are bivalved marine organisms. Although they resemble pelecypods, such as oysters, clams, and scallops, and some gastropods, such as slipper shells, they are not closely related. The three groups can be differentiated based on their planes of symmetry.

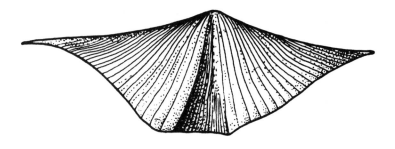

Cyrtospirifer disjunctus. **Devonian.** *(x 2)*

pelecypod

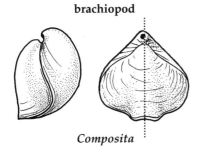

Mercenaria

brachiopod

Composita

gastropod

Crepidula

Lunatia

Pelecypod, brachiopod, gastropod. *Composita* sp. Mississippian. *Mercenaria* sp. Pliocene to Recent. *Crepidula* sp., slipper shell. Miocene to Recent. *Lunatia* sp., moon snail. Pleistocene to Recent.

Brachiopods *(Composita)* and pelecypods *(Mercenaria)* are bivalves, but the planes of symmetry are different. Gastropods are univalves, but some, such as slipper shells *(Crepidula),* may appear as one valve of a bivalve. The moon snail *(Lunatia)* is the more typical gastropod.

When looking directly at the top or bottom valves of a brachiopod, a line drawn through the midline will produce mirror images; the upper and lower valves themselves, however, are not mirror images of each other. Most brachiopods attached themselves to the seafloor by means of a fleshy stalk (pedicle) extended by the animal through one of its valves.

Brachiopod fossils are usually internal molds of the entire animal. As they used their muscles to open their valves, in death they remained closed. $(x\ ^3/_4)$

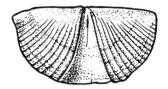

Spinocyrtia granulosa. **Devonian.**

MOLLUSKS
The mollusks include pelecypods, gastropods, scaphopods, cephalopods, and chitons (not discussed here).

Pelecypods
Pelecypods include scallops, oysters and clams. In most pelecypods, the top and bottom valves (left and right) are nearly identical, but each valve itself is not symmetrical. Oysters are the major exception in that the top and bottom valves may be very different in size. Pelecypod fossils are usually found as separate shells. They used their muscles to hold their valves together, and in death the valves usually separated. Cambrian to Recent.

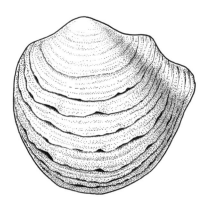

Pycnodonte mutabilis. **Cretaceous.** (*x* $^3/_5$)

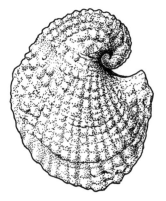

Exogyra costata. **Cretaceous.** (*x* $^1/_2$)

Ostrea falcata. **Cretaceous.**

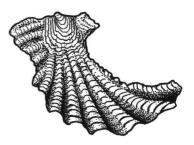

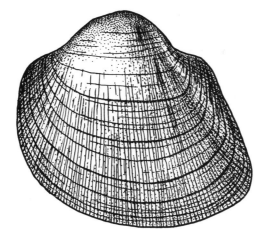

Cucullea gigantea. **Paleocene to Eocene. Shell.** $(x\ ^3/_8)$

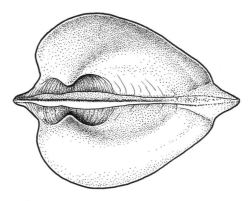

Cucullea gigantea. **Paleocene to Eocene. Internal mold, dorsal view.** $(x\ ^2/_5)$

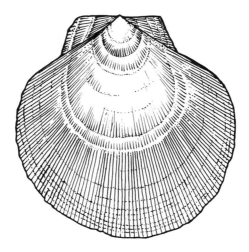

Placopecten clintonius. **Pliocene.** *(x 7/10)*

Gastropods

Gastropods include univalved animals such as slipper shells and snails, and the slugs, which have no shell. Most older gastropod fossils are internal molds. More recent fossils may be molds inside the original shells, and the most recent fossils may only be the shell. Cambrian to Recent.

internal mold   *shell*

Turritella mortoni. **Paleocene. Internal mold and shell.** *(x 3/4)*

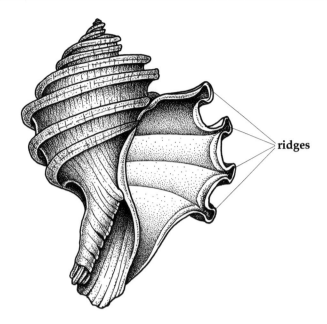

Ecphora gardnerae, **snail. Miocene. State fossil of Maryland. Similar to** *E. quadricostata* **(four ridges but not prominent) and** *E. tricostata* **(three prominent ridges).** *(x ³/₄)*

Scaphopods

Scaphopods, also known as tusk shells, are univalved and may resemble small teeth. Fossils may be molds or the original shells. Both ends were open, with the larger end planted in the seafloor. Ordovician to Recent.

Cadulus **sp., tusk shell. Eocene to recent.** *(x 2⁷/₁₀)*

Cephalopods

Cephalopods include the living octopuses, squids, cuttlefish, and nautiloids, as well as the extinct ammonites, baculites, and belemnites. The distinctive feature of nautiloids, ammonites, and baculites is the shell. Whether straight, coiled, or helical, the shell is composed of a series of chambers separated by thin walls, called septa. As the animal grew, it sealed off a chamber—leaving a small tube, or siphuncle, which linked the chambers and allowed the animal to control buoyancy—and produced a slightly larger chamber. The animal lived in only the last chamber.

The septal walls, at their contact with the outer shell, produced a pattern called a septal suture line. In life, an iridescent, mother-of-pearl layer coated the outside of the shell. In some specimens, this coating has remained; in many, it is not present and the suture patterns are evident.

Many nautiloid, ammonite, and baculite fossils are molds or casts; others were preserved with the internal structures intact. Casts of individual chambers of nautiloids, ammonites, and baculites are more frequent finds than the entire fossil.

Nautiloids

Nautiloids first appeared in the Cambrian and thrived in the Paleozoic. One genus with four species is still living. Paleozoic nautiloids were straight, but they eventually evolved into coiled forms. Their suture lines were straight and the living forms also exhibit straight sutures.

Michelinoceras **sp., straight nautiloid. Devonian.** *(x $^4/_5$)*

Hercoglossa twomeyi, coiled nautiloid. Eocene. *(x ²/₃)*

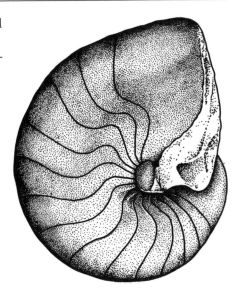

Ammonites

Ammonites first appeared in the Devonian and rose to prominence in the Mesozoic. The first ammonites had simple zigzag suture patterns. As they evolved, more elaborate and complicated suture patterns developed. It is believed that the more complex patterns gave more strength to the shell, allowing the animals to live in deeper water. They became extinct at the end of the Cretaceous.

Ammonite suture patterns, and thus the animals as well, are grouped into three broad categories:

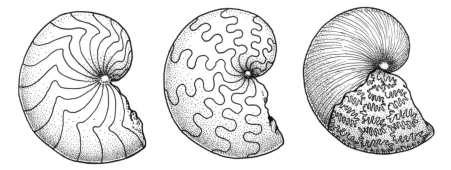

Left: Goniatite (first appeared in Devonian), *Tornoceras* **sp. Zigzag sutures. Center: Ceratite (first appeared in Mississippian),** *Agathiceras* **sp. Wavy sutures. Right: Ammonite (first appeared in Triassic),** *Phylloceras* **sp. Complex sutures.** *(x ⁷/₁₀)*

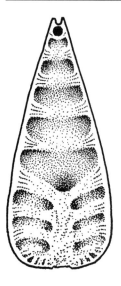

Placenticeras sp. Isolated single section, frontal view. *(x 2)*

Baculites

Baculites were straight ammonites with a small coil at one end. The coiled end is rarely preserved.

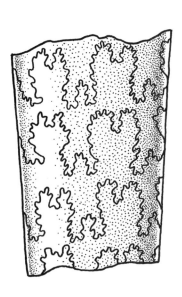

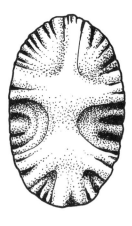

Baculites ovatus. Cretaceous. Lateral view (notice taper) and end view of one section.

Belemnites

Belemnites were squidlike and had no outer shell. Their remains are evidenced by the amber-colored, bullet-shaped internal structure, called a guard, which functioned like the cuttlebone of the living cuttlefish. They first appeared in the Carboniferous, but they thrived in the Jurassic and Cretaceous.

Belemnitella americana. Cretaceous. State fossil of Delaware. Internal guard. *(x ³/₅)*

STALKED ECHINODERMS

Crinoids

Crinoids are stalked echinoderms and are closely related to sea urchins, starfish, and sand dollars. They are commonly called sea lilies because of their flowerlike appearance, but they are animals (think of an upside-down starfish on a stalk). They first appeared in the Ordovician and some species still survive today. Nearly five thousand fossil species are known. Most spent their life attached to the seafloor in great colonies. The typical crinoid consisted of a root structure that held it to the seafloor, a segmented stalk, a crown (calyx) and branching arms, and sometimes armlets.

Eucalyptocrinites **sp. Mississippian.** *(x ³/₅)*

calyx

arm

plate

stem

columnal

holdfast (root)

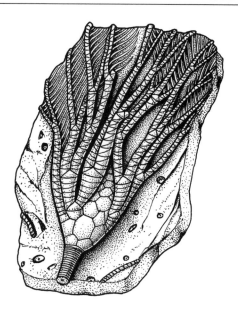

Blothrocrinus jesupi. **Mississippian.** *(x ²/₅)*

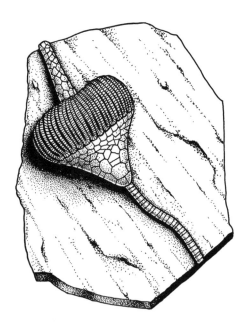

Eutrochocrinus christyi. **Mississippian.** *(x ³/₄)*

Columnals are pieces of crinoid stems, small disks that usually dissociated individually or in groups when an animal died. They are common finds. Native Americans frequently used them for ornamentation. Columnals. *(x 1¹/₅)*

Blastoids

Blastoids are also stalked echinoderms. The symmetrical crown was five-sided, and delicate arms radiated from it. The arms, stems, and roots are rarely preserved. Silurian to Permian.

Pentremites **sp., blastoid. Mississippian to Permian. Widespread, especially in Midwest. Side view.** *(x 2)*

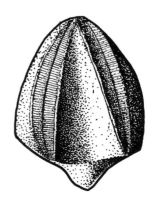

TRILOBITES

Trilobites were the dominant animals of the early Paleozoic. It is believed that they evolved from segmented worms. They appeared, fully formed, at the beginning of the Cambrian and were the first animals with complex (compound) eyes. They reached their peak, in terms of number of species, in the Cambrian, and then began a slow decrease in diversity until they were extinct by the end of the Permian. Nearly four thousand species have been identified.

Adult trilobites ranged in size from $1/4$ inch to 30 inches; most were $3/4$ to 3 inches. While there is great diversity in detail, the basic design changed little. Some species swam; others drifted, walked on the bottom, or plowed through sand or mud bottoms. All were confined to oceans.

Trilobites are named for the three longitudinal lobes that are separated by furrows. Trilobites also have three transverse sections separated by joints, encompassing the head (cephalon), thorax, and tail (pygidium).

The dorsal part of the exoskeleton was calcified, but the ventral portion, including the legs, was not. As a result, the undersides of trilobites rarely fossilized. Like all arthropods, trilobites had to molt to grow, and most fossils are shed skeletons and disarticulated pieces of shed skeletons. Other trilobite fossils are internal molds of dorsal skeletons. Most post-Cambrian trilobites could roll up in a ball, presumably for protection. Some trilobite fossils are found in the enrolled position.

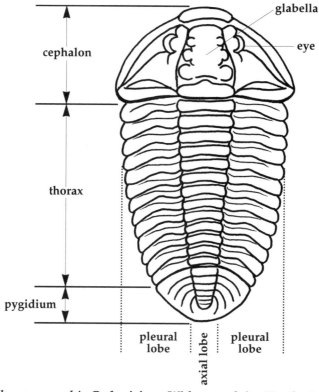

Flexicalymene meeki. **Ordovician. Widespread in North America. Semicircular head, tapered thorax, and small tail. Frequently found enrolled.** *(x 2)*

Elrathia kingii. Cambrian. Widespread in the West; state fossil of Utah. Small eyes, broadly oval and flattened body. *(x 2)*

Ceraurus pleurexanthemus. Ordovician. Widespread in North America. Oval to somewhat triangular. One of the more ornate types, with spines on the head, thorax, and tail. *(x 2)*

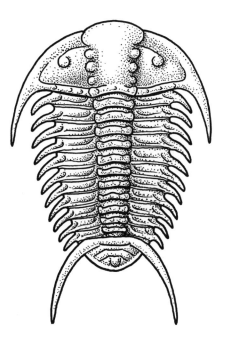

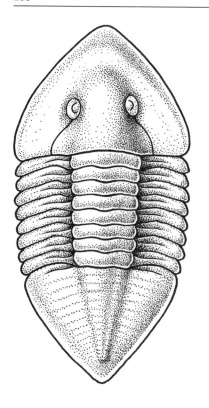

Isotelus gigas. Ordovician. Widespread in North America. Belongs to subfamily in which the middle lobe is less distinct.

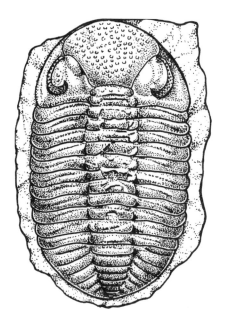

Phacops rana. Devonian. One of the best-known trilobites in North America. Oval, with large eyes. Frequently well preserved and often found enrolled. *(x 1⁴/₅)*

EURYPTERIDS

Eurypterids, although commonly called sea scorpions, lived in fresh, brackish, and salt water. Though they are found from the Ordovician to the Permian, they reached their zenith in the Silurian. Most species ranged in size from 6 inches to 18 inches, but *Pterygotus* reached 8 feet. It had strong pincers and was a formidable predator. If eurypterids are your quarry, New York is the state to hunt.

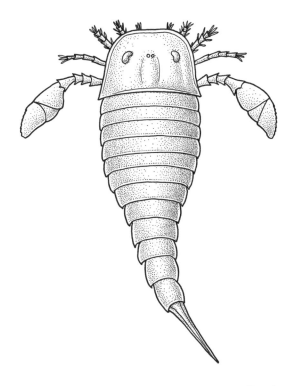

Eurypterus remipes, **eurypterid. Silurian. Generally about 8 inches long. State fossil of New York.** *(x ³/₄)*

Appendices

APPENDIX A

Fossil Exhibits

The following selected, nationwide fossil exhibits vary in size and specialty. Please contact the individual locations for more detailed information about their collections.

INDOORS

East

Massachusetts

Cambridge, Museum of Comparative Zoology, Harvard University

Connecticut

New Haven, Peabody Museum of Natural History, Yale University

New Jersey

Princeton, Princeton Natural History Museum

Trenton, New Jersey State Museum

New York

New York, American Museum of Natural History

Buffalo, Buffalo Museum of Science

North Carolina

Aurora, Aurora Fossil Museum

Pennsylvania

Philadelphia, Academy of Natural Sciences

Pittsburgh, Carnegie Museum of Natural History

District of Columbia

Washington, D.C., National Museum of Natural History (at the Smithsonian Institution)

Maryland

Solomons, Calvert Marine Museum

Florida

Tampa, Museum of Science and Industry

Gainesville, Florida Museum of Natural History

Bradenton, South Florida Museum

Mulberry, Mulberry Phosphate Museum

Central

Ohio

Cleveland, Cleveland Museum of Natural History

Illinois

Chicago, Field Museum of Natural History

South Dakota

Rapid City, Museum of Geology,

South Dakota School of Mines and Technology

Hill City, Black Hills Institute of Geological Research, Inc.

Nebraska

Lincoln, University of Nebraska State Museum

Crawford, Trailside Museum

Kansas

Hays, Sternberg Museum of Natural History

Texas

Houston, Houston Museum of Natural Science

Austin, Texas Memorial Museum

West

Montana

Bozeman, Museum of the Rockies

Wyoming

Kemmerer, Fossil Butte National Monument

East Thermopolis, Wyoming Dinosaur Center

Casper, Tate Minerological Museum, Casper College

Colorado

Denver, Denver Museum of Natural History

Grand Junction, Dinosaur Valley Museum

Utah

Vernal, Utah Field House of Natural History State Park

Salt Lake City, Utah Museum of Natural History

Price, College of Eastern Utah Prehistoric Museum

California

Los Angeles, George C. Page Museum of La Brea Discoveries

Los Angeles, Natural History Museum of Los Angeles County

Berkeley, Museum of Paleontology, University of California

Canada

Toronto, Ontario, Royal Ontario Museum

Drumheller, Alberta, Royal Tyrrell Museum of Paleontology

OUTDOORS

East

Connecticut

Rocky Hill, Dinosaur State Park

Central

South Dakota

Interior, Badlands National Park

Hot Springs, Mammoth Site of Hot Springs

Nebraska

Royal, Ashfall Fossil Beds State Park

Texas

Glen Rose, Dinosaur Valley State Park

West

Utah

Jenson, Dinosaur National Monument

Colorado

Florissant, Florissant Fossil Beds National Monument

Arizona

Holbrook, Petrified Forest National Park

Canada

Brooks, Alberta, Dinosaur Provincial Park

Major Fossil Shows

These are the major fossil shows, but you can contact local fossil and mineral clubs for smaller shows as well. In most cases, you will see the kinds of fossils that are found in your area, as well as fossils from places you may never get to visit.

Tucson Gem and Mineral Show
Tucson, Arizona
Early February
Contact: Tucson Gem and Mineral
  Society, Inc.
P.O. Box 42543
Tucson, AZ 85733
(602) 322-5773
The biggest gem, mineral, and fossil show in the world.

International Fossil Exposition
Macomb, Illinois
Mid-April
Contact: Mid-America Paleontology
  Society
4800 Sunset Dr. S.W.
Cedar Rapids, IA 52404
The biggest fossil-only show in the United States.

East Coast Gem, Mineral & Fossil Show
West Springfield, Massachusetts
Early August
Contact: Martin Zinn Expositions
P.O. Box 999
Evergreen, CO 80439
One of the larger multiaspect shows.

Denver Gem & Mineral Show
Denver, Colorado
Mid-September
Contact: Denver Gem & Mineral
  Show
P.O. Box 621444
Littleton, CO 80162
(303) 233-2516
One of the larger multiaspect shows.

Fossilmania

Glen Rose, Texas
Late October
Contact: Austin Paleontological Society
1603 Twilight Ridge
Austin, TX 78746
One of the biggest club shows.

Fossil Fair

Tampa, FL
Mid-March
Contact: Tampa Bay Fossil Club
P.O. Box 290561
Temple Terrace, FL 33687
One of the biggest club shows.

Phillips Auctioneers

New York, NY
June and December
Contact: Phillips Auctioneers
406 W. 79th St.
New York, NY 10021
(800) 825-ART1
The biggest natural history auctions in the United States.

Major Fossil Clubs

Don't despair if these clubs are not convenient. There are many others that can be found by contacting the geology department at a local college, the state Geological Survey, or science museums.

EAST

New York

The New York Paleontological Society
P.O. Box 287
Planetarium Station
127 W. 83rd St.
New York, NY 10024

Buffalo Geological Society, Inc.
Buffalo Museum of Science
Humboldt Parkway
Buffalo, NY 14211

New Jersey

New Jersey Paleontological Society
776 Asbury St.
New Milford, NJ 07646

Pennsylvania

Delaware Valley Paleontological Society
P.O. Box 686
Plymouth Meeting, PA 19462

Maryland

Maryland Geological Society
8052 Kavanagh Rd.
Baltimore, MD 21222

Calvert Marine Museum Fossil Club
P.O. Box 97
Solomons, MD 20688

North Carolina

North Carolina Fossil Club, Inc.
P.O. Box 2777
Durham, NC 27705

South Carolina

Myrtle Beach Fossil Club
Rt. 6
Box 269A
Conway, SC 29526

Florida

Bone Valley Fossil Society
2704 Dixie Rd.
Lakeland, FL 33801

Florida Fossil Hunters
320 W. Rich Ave.
Deland, FL 32272

Florida Paleontological Society
Florida Museum of Natural History
University of Florida
Gainsville, FL 32611

Fossil Club of Miami
12540 S.W. 37th St.
Miami, FL 33175

Southwest Florida Fossil Club
P.O. Box 151651
Cape Coral, FL 33915

Tampa Bay Fossil Club
P.O. Box 290561
Temple Terrace, FL 33687

CENTRAL

Ohio

Dry Dredgers
Deparment of Geology
University of Cincinnati
Cincinnati, OH 45221

Cleveland Museum of Natural History
1 Wade Oval University Circle
Cleveland, OH 44106

Illinois

Earth Science Club of Northern Illinois
Paleontology Group
Box 321
Downers Grove, IL 60515

Michigan

Friends of the University of Michigan
Museum of Paleontology, Inc.
University of Michigan
1109 Geddes Rd.
Ann Arbor, MI 48109

Missouri

Eastern Missouri Society for Paleontology
P.O. Box 21045
Normandy, MO 63121

Iowa

The Mid-America Paleontological Society
4800 Sunset Dr. S.W.
Cedar Rapids, IA 52404

Texas

Austin Paleontological Society
1603 Twilight Ridge
Austin, TX 78746

Dallas Paleontological Society
P.O. Box 710265
Dallas, TX 75371

Houston Gem & Mineral Society
Paleontology Section
10805 Brooklet
Houston, TX 77099

WEST

Colorado

Western Interior Paleontological Society
P.O. Box 200011
Denver, CO 80220

California

Southern California Paleontological Society

1826 Ninth St.
Manhattan Beach, CA 90266

The Fossils for Fun Society, Inc.
1449 Sebastian Way
Sacramento, CA 95864

The San Diego Mineral and Gem Society
Fossil Division
Gem and Mineral Bldg., Balboa Park
San Diego, CA 92101

Collecting Sites

The following are well-known collecting sites that continue to regularly produce fossils—sometimes even significant specimens. Except where noted, access is free and you may keep what you find. However, access and regulations may change at any time, so check ahead before you plan a trip.

NEW YORK

PENN DIXIE QUARRY, HAMBURG
DEVONIAN FOSSILS

In 1990, this site was headed for ruin, at least as far as fossil collecting is concerned, as commercial development was close at hand. A mixture of public and local governmental support spearheaded by the nonprofit Hamburg Natural History Society resulted in the purchase of these 32 acres by the town of Hamburg (southwest of Buffalo). The society administers the site and runs public-access days once a month from spring until fall.

This site is a great place to collect. It is flat, and the trilobites, cephalopods, brachiopods, crinoids, corals, bryozoans, and even fish fossils are literally weathering out of the shale at your feet! You will go home with an instant middle Devonian collection. Because the fossils are so plentiful, this is one of the few collecting sites where you will not hear the phrase "You should have been here ten years ago."

Take along a hammer, a chisel, and a big bucket. The society charges $3 admission for adults and $2 for children. Membership in the society is not required, but it's a nice way to support its efforts. For information, contact Hamburg Natural History Society, Box 772, Hamburg, NY 14075.

NEW JERSEY

WALTER KIDDE DINOSAUR PARK AT RIKER HILL, ROSEMONT
LATE TRIASSIC/EARLY JURASSIC DINOSAUR TRACKS

This site is on the side of a hill with an apartment complex at the base. The site is not for the casual collector. Take sledgehammers, mauls, hammers, chisels, heavy-duty gloves, and short-handled brooms or stiff brushes. Be prepared to break and split a lot of rock. The most frequent finds are theropod dinosaur tracks, but you'll also find mud cracks, ripple marks, and an occasional insect trail.

The problem with any track site is that it's often difficult to discern tracks at first glance (or second or third, for that matter). Occasionally, tracks are recovered from discard piles when collectors were not careful about what they threw away. Spring and early fall are the best times to visit. Otherwise, you'll be at the mercy of temperature extremes, bugs, and leaf clutter.

Directions: From the Garden State Parkway in northern New Jersey, exit west onto I-280. Take Exit 5B and head north on N. Livingston/Roseland. Turn left onto Route 520/Eagle Rock. Just before you reach Eisenhower Parkway, there will be a dirt road on your left. Turn left onto the dirt road, and drive until you reach a parking lot on your left. Opposite the parking lot, and on the right side of the dirt road, is a trail that leads to the site. An apartment complex is to the left, and the hill is to the right. You may need to go up the hill to where the quarrying activity is obvious.

BIG BROOK, MONMOUTH COUNTY
LATE CRETACEOUS VERTEBRATE MATERIAL

This is a classic streambed site. The remains of everything from Cretaceous mosasaurs and plesiosaurs to Pleistocene mammals can be found here. The most prevalent finds are Cretaceous shark teeth. On occasion, arrowheads and colonial artifacts have been found.

Take long-handled shovels and box screens. To use a box screen, lay it on the bank or in shallow water, drop a few shovelfuls of stream-bottom material into the screen, rinse it in the water, and see what you've got—it's addicting. In the summer, it's pleasant, and you can slosh through the water in a pair of old tennis shoes; cooler weather requires insulated hip waders. Local fossil clubs traditionally have "polar bear" field trips in midwinter.

Directions: From Freehold, New Jersey, head north on State Route 79. Turn right onto Route 520 (going east). Travel about 1 mile, and turn right onto Boundary Road. Travel about 1 mile to where it crosses Big Brook. Park safely along the road, head downstream, and start collecting. As of this writing, upstream is posted.

MARYLAND

CALVERT CLIFFS, CALVERT COUNTY
MIOCENE MARINE FOSSILS

An 18-mile stretch of the western shore of the Chesapeake Bay, from Chesapeake Beach in the north to Solomons Island at the southern terminus, Calvert Cliffs is one of the premier sites in the world for Miocene marine fossils. At any given time, shark teeth, porpoise, and whale remains are easily found by strolling along the beach. During the summer, fossils are harder to come by because of the many collectors who visit the area.

The best collecting is an hour or two before or after low tide. In the summer, you can go barefoot (wear old tennis shoes with knee-high socks to avoid jellyfish if you plan to wade in the water). Cooler water temperatures demand insulated waders. The best time of the year to collect is in the winter, several days after a big storm. Remember, the reason fossils are abundant on the beach is that parts of the cliffs fall down from time to time. So reread chapter 7, and don't even think about climbing the cliffs!

Directions: Unfortunately, there are only three public-access sites—Calvert Cliffs State Park, Flag Ponds Nature Park, and Matoaka Cottages—but if you ask around, you may find some additional access points. All three sites are accessible from State Route 2-4, which parallels the western side of the Chesapeake Bay. Calvert Cliffs State Park is approximately 5 miles north of Solomons, Maryland. There are signs along Route 2-4, and there is parking, but it is a nearly 2-mile hike to the beach. Flag Ponds Nature Park is approximately 9 miles north of Solomons. Look for the signs on Route 2-4. There is parking and a 1/2-mile walk to the beach. Matoaka Cottages is privately owned. To reach it from Route 2-4, head east on Calvert Beach Road, which is about 3 miles north of Flag Ponds. Go through the town of St. Leonard and then 1.3 miles farther until you reach the sign for Matoaka. Bear left onto the dirt road, and continue until you reach the cottages (about 3/4 mile). Matoaka is the only one of the three sites that is open all year. There is a nominal parking fee.

FLORIDA

VENICE BEACH
MIOCENE AND PLIOCENE SHARK TEETH

Small to medium-size Miocene shark teeth are abundant here. In fact, the best place on earth to find fossil shark teeth on any given day is Venice Beach. You won't be alone, but chances are you will still find teeth. A scooper of hard wire mesh or soft netting will help you sift through the sand in an upright position instead of having to bend over to hunt for these treasures. As with any Florida site, take along sunscreen and a hat. Try getting out early in the morning or at low tide to lessen the competition.

Experienced scuba divers should check with local dive shops, which can direct you to the offshore area where the teeth originate. Bigger teeth are frequently found by divers.

THE PALEO PRESERVE, RUSKIN
EARLY PLEISTOCENE LAND ANIMALS

Throughout the 1980s, the Leisey Shell Pit, south of Tampa Bay, became the most famous early Pleistocene site in the world, with nearly 150 species of animals, some of them new to science, being found. In 1995, a nonprofit corporation, The Paleontological Education Preserve, was created with the purpose of educating area schoolchildren and adults about fossils and paleontology. Membership is available in the Paleo Preserve for a nominal fee, which, in addition to other benefits, allows access to the site on member dig days. You may keep anything you find, unless it is scientifically significant.

Take along a hat, sunscreen, and digging tools. Who knows what will turn up on any given day, but mastodon, mammoth, saber-toothed cat, giant sloth, camel, and many other exotic Ice Age finds await you. For information about membership and collecting, contact The Paleontological Education Preserve, 223 Third St. N., Suite 204, St. Petersburg, FL 33701, telephone (813) 898-7409.

PEACE RIVER, ARCADIA
MIOCENE TO PLEISTOCENE MARINE AND LAND ANIMALS

The Southeast is noted for productive river and ocean areas of Miocene, Pliocene, and Pleistocene fossils. At many of these sites, however, the water may be cloudy or silty, and the currents strong. The Peace River, in central Florida, has the best combination of fossil collecting and low (water-based) risk. Large cypress trees with Spanish moss line the river. Common birds include herons, egrets, ibis, kingfishers, and birds of prey.

Reptilian fauna includes turtles, snakes, and an occasional alligator and can be somewhat unnerving at first.

The best way to collect is to rent a canoe from Canoe Outpost and paddle up- or downriver. The river is tannin-stained but clear. It is quite shallow (1 to 3 feet) for most of its length, except for the occasional deep pocket of water. The current is generally slow. Collecting is best from late fall to early spring, when water levels are low and the water is clearest. Look for areas of small, black phosphate pebbles in the bottom sediment, beach the canoe, and wade in the shallow water. Fossils may be obvious, or you may need to fan the silt. Sport sandals or old tennis shoes are recommended. Consider snorkeling in the deeper areas.

Common finds include shark teeth, sea cow ribs, pieces of turtle shell, and, to a lesser extent, mastodon and mammoth material. In 1996, an amateur collector found a nearly complete mammoth skeleton in the river right next to the campground!

Directions: From Tampa, take I-75 south and exit onto State Route 70 East south of Bradenton. Head east to the intersection of Route 70 and County Road 661, which is just before the Peace River and the town of Arcadia. The Peace River Campground is at this intersection. Turn left onto County Road 661, and follow the signs to Canoe Outpost. If you enjoy camping, the Peace River Campground is ideal.

ILLINOIS

Mazon Creek, Godley
Pennsylvanian plant and invertebrate concretions

The Mazon Creek site is famous for the more than four hundred species of plants and animals from the Pennsylvanian period, about 290 million years ago, that have been found there. Fossils may be collected from the spoil piles around the lake, which is used to cool the nearby Braidwood Nuclear Plant. The piles can be accessed on foot or by boat. All of the fossils are found inside concretions that weather out from the spoils. The concretions may be round, elliptical, or flattened. Nearly 80 percent of all concretions have something inside. Of that 80 percent, about 20 percent contain something recognizable—mostly plant and invertebrate species, although vertebrates are occasionally found.

The best collecting strategy is to go up and down the spoil piles, picking up concretions. Pay close attention to the valleys and gullies created by erosion. One of the unique aspects of collecting here is that you may not learn what you have found for several years, because the best way to open the concretions is not to break them open, but to allow them to freeze and thaw repeatedly during the winter.

Place them in a bucket of water, leave them outside in the cold for several days to freeze, and then bring them inside to thaw. Repeat the process throughout the winter. Eventually, the concretions will crack, almost always along the plane of the fossil inside. This method is certainly not for the eager collector, but it's a nice way to remember your time there for years to come.

A permit is required to collect and can be obtained by contacting Dr. Chris Ledvina, Northeastern Illinois University, 5500 N. St. Louis Ave., Chicago, IL 60625. The free permit, directions, and regulations will be sent to you.

TEXAS

Brazos and Little Brazos Rivers, Stone City
Eocene marine fossils

This is an excellent location for Eocene shells and, to a lesser extent, shark teeth and bony fish material. These are riverbank sites along the Little Brazos and Brazos Rivers where they are crossed by State Route 21. The shells are obvious and are in several clay layers that run about $1/2$ mile upstream and down from the Route 21 bridges.

Collecting is best when the water levels are low. The Little Brazos is shallow enough to walk in, so check the streambed and the banks. The Brazos is deep, so you'll be able to collect only along the banks. A walking stick will help you at both sites. A screwdriver or knife is necessary to dig the fossils out of the matrix, and a bucket is useful for carrying them. The clay can be removed more easily if the fossils are allowed to dry.

Directions: From Bryan, Texas, head southwest on State Route 21 until it reaches the Little Brazos River. The Brazos is about 2 miles farther. You can park along the road and walk down the banks at both rivers. Keep an eye out for spiders and snakes.

High Island
Pleistocene land animal and marine fossils

Pleistocene vertebrate material and shells can be found on this classic beach surface-collecting site east of the town of High Island. There is about a 20-mile stretch of beach that you can walk. It's best to collect at low tide, as the fossils are eroding out of a formation offshore. Collecting after a storm can sometimes result in excellent finds.

Directions: High Island can be reached by taking the ferry from Galveston or by heading east on I-10 from Houston and exiting south onto State Route 124. You can park along the side of the road.

TEXAS CITY DIKE, TEXAS CITY
PLEISTOCENE LAND MAMMAL AND MARINE FOSSILS

The Texas City Dike is a man-made structure that extends some 5 miles from Texas City into the Houston ship channel. The foundation of the dike was made of dredgings from nearby areas that contain Pleistocene fossils. The dike itself has a road and is commercialized, with small stores and bait shops. Fossils can be found on the banks of the dike. It's also a popular place to fish.

Directions: Texas City is just north of Galveston and east of I-45. Leave I-45 at Exit 10, head east on State Route 519, and follow signs to the dike.

WYOMING

ULRICH'S FOSSIL QUARRIES, KEMMERER
EOCENE FISH

Fossil collectors from all over the world are familiar with the beautifully preserved Eocene fossil fish from the Green River Formation of southwestern Wyoming. The quarry is near the Fossil Butte National Monument. Unlike the monument, the quarry is privately owned and allows the public to collect (for a fee) and keep any common fossils found. "Rare and unusual" finds, as designated by the state of Wyoming, may not be retained.

The shale was formed 55 million years ago at the bottom of a freshwater lake that occupied the area. The layers of shale resemble pages of a book. When the pages are opened, or split apart, the specimens are apparent, as the vertebral column stands out from the compressed body.

The quarry, which is at an elevation of 7,200 feet, is open only from June 1 through Labor Day, and advance reservations are required. The $55 fee includes transportation into and out of the quarry, all necessary tools and equipment, and trimming the shale that holds your finds. A staff member accompanies all groups.

A brochure describing the quarry, the services, rules and regulations, and directions can be obtained by contacting Ulrich's Fossil Quarries, Fossil Station #308, Kemmerer, WY 83101, telephone (307) 877-6466.

Dinosaur Digs

If you've caught dinosaur fever, you have money to spare, and you don't mind not keeping what you find, there are a number of hunting and excavation trips available. This is merely a listing of sponsors and should not be construed as an endorsement of the sponsors or their expeditions.

Dinamation International Society
550 Crossroads Court
Fruita, CO 81521
(800) 344-3466

Earthwatch
680 Mount Auburn St.
P.O. Box 403
Watertown, MA
(617) 926-8200

Museum of the Rockies
Montana State University
Bozeman, MT 59717
(406) 994-6618

Royal Tyrrell Musuem of Paleontology
Box 7500
Drumheller, Alberta T0J 0Y0
Canada
(403) 823-7707

Smithsonian Institution
Smithsonian Study Tours and Seminars
1100 Jefferson Dr., S.W., MRC702
Washington, DC 20560
(202) 357-4700

University Research Expeditions Program
University of California
Berkeley, CA 94720
(510) 642-6586

APPENDIX

F

Suggested Reading

GENERAL INFORMATION ABOUT FOSSILS

The Fossil Book, by Carroll L. Fenton and Mildred A. Fenton (New York: Double-day, 1989). A little bit about almost everything.

Vertebrate Paleontology and Evolution, by Robert L. Carroll (New York: W. H. Free-man and Co., 1988). Bible for those with an academic interest in vertebrate paleontology.

The Macmillan Illustrated Encyclopedia of Dinosaurs and Prehistoric Animals, by Dou-gal Dixon, Barry Cox, R. J. G. Savage, and Brian Gardiner (New York: Macmil-lan, 1988). Color illustrations and summaries about dinosaurs and many other interesting vertebrates.

Fossil Invertebrates, eds. Richard S. Boardman, Alan H. Cheetham, and Albert J. Rowell (Boston: Blackwell Scientific Publications, 1987). Bible for those with an academic interest in invertebrate paleontology.

A Pictorial Guide to Fossils, by Gerard R. Case (New York: Van Nostrand Reinhold, 1982). Nearly thirteen hundred photographs and illustrations of fossils.

The Encyclopedia of Pre-Historic Life, eds. Rodney Steel and Anthony Harvey (New York: McGraw-Hill, 1979). A vast amount of information in alphabetical form.

SPECIFIC FOSSIL TOPICS

Fossil Diving, by Bob Sinibaldi (Palm Harbor, FL: IBIS Graphics, 1998). The first book to focus on underwater collecting of fossils.

Vertebrate Fossils: A Neophyte's Guide, by Frank A. Kocsis, Jr. (Palm Harbor, FL: IBIS Graphics, 1997). More than eight hundred photographs of Miocene, Pliocene, and Pleistocene vertebrate fossils.

208

Discovering Fossil Fishes, by John G. Maisey (New York: Henry Holt, 1996). For the beginner and the advanced amateur.

Amber: Window to the Past, by David A. Grimaldi (New York: Harry N. Abrams, 1996). A wonderful coffee-table book with photographs of some of the most unusual inclusions in amber.

Cretaceous and Paleogene Fossils of North Carolina, by John Timmerman and Richard Chandler (available through North Carolina Fossil Club, P.O. Box 2777, Durham, NC 27705, 1995). An excellent field guide, not just for North Carolina.

Neogene Fossils of North Carolina, by John Timmerman and Richard Chandler (available through North Carolina Fossil Club, P.O. Box 2777, Durham, NC 27705, 1994). Another excellent field guide.

Fossil Sharks of the Chesapeake Bay Region, by Bretton W. Kent (Columbia, MD: Egan Rees & Boyer, 1994). Everything you need to know about Miocene and other fossil sharks—not just for this area.

Mammoths, by Adrian Lister and Paul Bahn (New York: Macmillan, 1994). The last word on mammoths, for now.

The Collector's Guide to Fossil Sharks and Rays from the Cretaceous of Texas, by Bruce J. Welton and Roger F. Farish (Lewisville, TX: Before Time, 1993). Excellent photographs and information, for Cretaceous sharks and rays anywhere.

The Velvet Claw: A Natural History of the Carnivores, by David Macdonald (London: BBC Books, 1992). An excellent resource for living and extinct carnivores. A companion book to the BBC television series.

Life in Amber, by George O. Poinar, Jr. (Stanford, CA: Stanford University Press, 1992). More text than photographs, but well worth reading.

Cretaceous Fossils from the Chesapeake and Delaware Canal, by Edward M. Lauginiger (Newark, DE: Delaware Geological Survey Special Publication No. 18, 1988). An excellent guide to Cretaceous marine fossils—not just for Delaware.

Mammalian Evolution: An Illustrated Guide, by R. J. G. Savage and M. R. Long (New York: Facts on File, 1986). Lots of good information.

Trilobites: A Photographic Atlas, by Riccardo Levi-Setti (Chicago: University of Chicago Press, 1975). Photographs of many trilobites.

The White River Badlands, by Cleophas C. O'Harra (Rapid City, SD: South Dakota School of Mines, Bulletin No. 13, 1920). Yes, 1920, and it's still the best book about the fossils of the Badlands.

FOSSIL SITES AND MUSEUMS

Old Stones and Serpent Bones, vols. 1 and 2, by T. Skwara (Blacksburg, VA: McDonald & Woodward Publishing Company, 1992). Eighty-five sites in the United States and Canada—look but don't touch.

Dinosaur Safari Guide: Tracking North America's Prehistoric Past, by Vincenzo Costa (Stillwater, MN: Voyageur Press, 1994). A guide to, predominantly, dinosaur sites and exhibits in the United States and Canada.

Fossil Collecting in the Mid-Atlantic States, by Jasper Burns (Baltimore: Johns Hopkins University Press, 1991). The best guide to collecting sites ever published. Superb illustrations.

PALEONTOLOGICAL TECHNIQUES

Vertebrate Paleontological Techniques, eds. Patrick Leiggi and Peter May (Cambridge: Cambridge University Press, 1994).

Handbook of Paleo-preparation Techniques, by Howard H. Converse, Jr. (Gainesville, FL: Florida Paleontological Society, 1989).

GENERAL SKELETAL ANATOMY

Skulls and Bones, by Glen Searfoss (Mechanicsburg, PA: Stackpole Books, 1995). Skeletal line drawings of present-day animals.

Bones: The Unity of Form and Function, by R. McNeill Alexander (New York: Macmillan, 1994). A superbly photographed coffee-table book with informative text.

Skeleton, by Steve Parker (New York: Alfred A. Knopf, 1988). An Eyewitness Book; well photographed and full of useful information.

OUTDOOR FIRST AID

National Outdoor Leadership School's Wilderness First Aid, by Tod Schimelpfenig and Linda Lindsey (Harrisburg, PA: Stackpole Books, 1991).

Outward Bound Wilderness First-Aid Handbook, by Jeff Isaac and Peter Goth (New York: Lyons & Burford Publishers, 1991).

MAGAZINES AND PERIODICALS

To keep up with the latest developments, check out these publications, available at most libraries or bookstores.

Discover, published by Walt Disney Publications Group (New York).

Earth, published by Kalmbach Publishing Company (Waukesha, WI).

Geotimes, published by American Geological Institute (Alexandria, VA).

Lapidary Journal, published by Lapidary Journal, Inc. (Devon, PA).

National Geographic, published by National Geographic Society (Washington, DC).

Natural History, published by American Museum of Natural History (New York, NY).

Smithsonian, published by Smithsonian Associates (Washington, DC).

Index

Page numbers in italics indicate illustrations.